THE

How to Build, Scale, and Sell Your Canadian Mortgage Business

BUSINESS OF BROKERING

DOUG ADLAM, MSc.

Published by Prominence Publishing.

The Business of Brokering / Adlam, Doug. -- 1st ed.

Paperback ISBN: 978-1-997649-17-5

Hardcover ISBN: 978-1-997649-03-8

Table of Contents

What People Are Saying

Forever a consummate professional who wears his heart on his sleeve. Having known Doug for nearly a dozen years now, he is not just an industry colleague, but has become a close friend. His ability to truly connect with people on a personal level has translated into forging lasting friendships and solid industry partnerships. Fitting that we hit it off at our first introduction, in a Mortgage Mastermind Group together, the topic of discussion: 'The Entrepreneur's Journey'. Fast forward to today, Doug is providing guidance from real world experience with the stripes and scars earned along the way.

Scott H. Bentley

***

Doug is the kind of leader our industry needs more of, visionary, grounded, and generous with his knowledge. He brings that lived experience with such clarity and honesty. His ability to turn complex challenges into actionable strategies makes him a trusted voice, not just in mortgages but in business. This book reflects his rare ability to inspire while offering practical, proven strategies.

Michelle Campbell

***

WHAT PEOPLE ARE SAYING

Doug distills the essence of mortgage brokering and shows how to build a thriving business within a complex ecosystem, delivered in a clear, easy-to-read style. A must-read for anyone exploring a career in mortgage brokering, and a valuable checkpoint for established brokers and owners to assess whether they truly own a business or are simply trading time for money.

Dan Putnam

***

As a successful brokerage owner who has had the pleasure of collaborating on many topics over the years with Doug, I can confidently say that this book on Building a Mortgage Business offers great insights for anyone looking to venture into this space.

Kerri Reed

***

Doug's The Business of Brokering is a game-changer for mortgage professionals, offering clear, battle-tested strategies forged from his years of building a thriving mortgage business and investing in fintech. As a long-time colleague and close friend, I've witnessed his sharp insight and relentless drive firsthand. This book captures that brilliance, delivering practical wisdom for creating lasting success. This Blueprint is an essential read for anyone serious about elevating their game in the industry.

Tom Gasparec

***

I've known Doug Adlam as a colleague and close friend for years and have always been impressed by his incredible insight into the mortgage industry. With The Business of Brokering, he has distilled his decades of experience—from founding an award-winning brokerage to co-founding a groundbreaking fintech company—into a truly invaluable guide. This book isn't just about the mechanics of the job; it's a strategic roadmap for building a business that creates lasting value. It's a must-read for any mortgage professional ready to take their career to the next level.

Rob Cagnin

***

The journey of a mortgage professional can feel like a solo journey - but it doesn't have to be. Doug has created a lighthouse in this book: a guide lit by real stories, raw truths, and the kind of wisdom that only comes from walking the walk. Whether you are just starting out or wondering what comes next, The Business of Brokering offers the clarity, courage, and heart we all need to keep going and keep growing as mortgage professionals.

Frances Hinojosa

***

Doug Adlam is a kind, trailblazing leader who has always put others first. His dedication to the mortgage brokering world and his willingness to share knowledge and support others shines through in this book. The Business of Brokering is not just a guide, it's a reflection of Doug's generosity and commitment to helping our industry thrive.

Nick L'Ecuyer

***

The Business of Brokering fills a critical gap in our industry, offering brokers a clear roadmap to build businesses that are sustainable and saleable—not just short-term jobs. If you want to create a business you can one day sell, rather than simply work until you can't anymore, this book is an indispensable guide.

Veronica Love

***

The Business of Brokering, is the essential Doug Adlam. It is rare in life and in business, where one's stated beliefs are actually what has transpired. Having worked alongside Doug, as well as watching him grow as a leading edge mortgage professional and entrepreneur in our industry at large, Doug is the real deal, and most definitely walks the walk, that he describes in his book. This is a must read for any mortgage broker or for any business owner at any stage, in their development, or looking to level up their business.

Gord Dahlen

***

As a Brokerage Owner, I found The Business of Brokering offers a thoughtful and accurate perspective on the Mortgage Brokerage business and the creation of value. Doug brings unique experiences and insights as a Leader and Entrepreneur in the Canadian Mortgage Industry.

Don MacVicar

***

Doug Adlam is a smart, forward-thinking leader whose mastery of technology, systems, and people makes this book a must-read.

Eitan Pinsky

***

I've had the privilege of knowing Doug for years, watching him move from the planning stages of ideas right through to executing successful businesses. His book, The Business of Brokering, perfectly reflects the wisdom, systems, and entrepreneurial mindset he's lived out in our industry. As both a colleague and a friend, I can say with confidence that Doug's insights are invaluable for anyone serious about building a mortgage business with longevity and purpose.

James Loewen

***

I've had the pleasure of knowing Doug for several years, and working with him has always been a true partnership. As he shares in The Business of Brokering, real success in this industry comes from building meaningful, strategic relationships rooted in trust and collaboration. That message resonates deeply with me, as it reflects the very foundation of how Doug and I have worked together over the years. This book is not just a guide for brokers, but an inspiring reminder of the power of relationships in building something lasting.

Elena Robinson

***

The Business of Brokering is a masterclass in both business and sales strategy, written with a clarity that only comes from deep, hands-on experience. Doug Adlam has an exceptional ability to break down complex concepts into practical insights that brokers and entrepreneurs alike can immediately apply. What sets this book apart is that he doesn't just teach tactics—he inspires a mindset of professionalism, growth, and collaboration that aims to strengthen the industry as a whole.

Gordon Ross

***

Doug Adlam is a veteran and expert in the mortgage industry in Canada. He brings that expertise, together with his entrepreneurial spirit, teaching mastery and knowledge of the technology sector into a must read for mortgage professionals at all levels of their career and anyone else looking to learn about the industry.

Bruno Valko

***

This is an exceptional book that delivers insight-driven strategies for achieving industry-leading performance. With 17 years of experience, a thriving brokerage, and deep expertise in the mortgage industry, Doug provides invaluable guidance to mortgage brokers and agents at every stage of their careers. Having personally witnessed the growth of his brokerage from its early days to the success it is today, I can confidently say this book is grounded in real-world experience and proven tactics—essential reading for anyone in the industry or looking to enter it.

Sandra Calla (Carano)

***

Building a sustainable mortgage business is difficult. Doug speaks to the missteps and pitfalls of many who run their business with their head down – short term success, long term struggles. Learn to do things with intentionality and build a valuable business.

Dong Lee

***

I've known Doug for over 15 years. He's a friend, colleague, and leader - someone I always look to for something new. This book is something new. A refreshing take on the journey of mortgage brokering from start to finish.

Chris Horrocks

***

After coaching thousands of mortgage professionals over two decades, Doug Adlam stands out as both my most successful student and most influential leader. His superpower? Taking complex strategies and distilling them into simple, actionable steps that create lasting freedom. Doug doesn't just teach—he lives these principles, and his results prove it works. If you want the proven blueprint for building a mortgage business that truly sets you free, this is your roadmap.

Doren Aldana

***

I saw Doug bring crucial insight, network, and Go-To-Market drive to launch our industry disrupting Fintech. This book carries the same DNA — a hard-won playbook for building a mortgage business that grows beyond you.

Johnny Watson

***

Doug Adlam's The Business of Brokering is a practical, strategic blueprint for mortgage professionals who want to build businesses that outlast them. Drawing on 17+ years of experience, this book will transform a salesperson mindset to true ownership: purposeful planning, repeatable systems, intentional hiring, and exceptional client value. Doug's clear guidance on choosing focus, building culture, leveraging partnerships, and planning exit strategies makes complex decisions actionable. Whether scaling, leading teams, or preparing to sell, brokers, lenders, and industry leaders will find honest, unbiased advice that creates transferable, long-term value. Essential reading for anyone serious about building a saleable mortgage business.

Anna DeMarco

***

Doug has managed to turn years of hard-won experience into a book that's as practical as it is inspiring. The Business of Brokering doesn't just explain how to run a brokerage—it gives you the blueprint to build, grow, and eventually exit with confidence. This is the kind of resource every broker wishes they had when starting out.

Myles Nowik

***

Adlam's book is not just a "must read", it's an essential tool for mortgage pros who wish to scale their business beyond just a transactional client list. The difference between simply providing oneself a job and building a scalable and saleable business, is clear in the pages of this experience driven read. As a 25-year veteran of the Canadian mortgage industry, I am of the opinion this is a highly worthy outline of the thought process and planning required to move from being just one of the herd, to a trusted go-to brand throughout the mortgage life cycle. Two thumbs up!

Adrian McInerney

***

What sets Doug apart is not only his technical expertise but also his dedication to coaching and developing others. Whether dealing directly with clients or mentoring professionals in the industry, Doug leads with integrity, patience, and a genuine commitment to helping people succeed.

Scott Wittrup

***

The Business of Brokering is an essential resource for mortgage professionals aiming to build a sustainable, scalable and successful business. Doug Adlam imparts his wealth of experience through a powerful blueprint that transitions brokers from mere salespeople to savvy entrepreneurs. Filled with actionable insights on planning, growth, and exit strategies, this indispensable resource equips mortgage professionals at every stage to build a thriving and sustainable business.

Trupti Patel

***

This book is the blueprint for brokers ready to stop trading hours for dollars and start building a modern, thriving mortgage business.

Carter Zimmerman

***

The Business of Brokering is long overdue in the mortgage industry. As the industry continues to evolve, capture market share, and grow stronger, more brokers need to start viewing their mortgage practice as an asset—not just a job. Too many still operate with a transactional mindset, focused only on the deal in front of them. This book challenges that approach and provides the framework to shift toward building a long-term, sustainable business—one that creates real value, equity, and legacy.

Russ Morrison

***

Doug is a highly talented broker who is on top of his game! The Business of Brokering is a must read for both new and experienced mortgage professionals who are serious about taking their career to the next level.

Paul Meredith

***

WHAT PEOPLE ARE SAYING

Having built and exited my own mortgage business, I know how vital it is to design a mortgage business with the end in mind. In The Business of Brokering, Doug brings clarity and strategy to that process, providing a practical roadmap for brokers who want to move beyond chasing files and instead create a scalable, saleable business that delivers freedom, value, and lasting legacy.

Penny Wrightly

***

The Business of Brokering is a much-needed review of how to treat mortgage brokering like a business...something that has been lacking for a long time. Too often, new agents get stuck putting out fires and never move to the next level. This book provides them with the roadmap to grow the right pieces for long-term success.

Mike Lloyd

***

A necessary read from a brilliant mind. Mortgage professionals from all ends of the profession will benefit from this book. Adding strategy to one's business model and thinking past the immediate transaction can and will transform any professional's business positively. Regardless of the stage of one's career, this book is unmistakably applicable and it's a bonus that it's written by someone with a proven track record of success multiple times over.

Taylor Lewis

***

In my career, Doug has always been a beacon of entrepreneurial energy and deep industry knowledge. In The Business of Brokering he delivers his most essential mortgage brokering insights as a concise, action-oriented guide. It's a must-read for any broker looking to grow.

Tom Hall

***

Doug's experience in the mortgage industry, across multiple different roles, gives him the unique ability to provide an ideal framework for Brokers, both new and experienced, to lean on when building and scaling their businesses. This book is sure to provide long-term value to anyone who reads it.

Jeff Ingram

***

In The Business of Brokering, Doug Adlam distills years of hands-on brokering, hard earned learnings and leadership experience into proven strategies that are both practical and transformative to drive real results. More than just a guide, it's a thoughtful blueprint for brokers at any stage, offering insights that inspire confidence and equip readers with tools to achieve meaningful, lasting success.

Marnie George

***

Doug Adlam is a proven leader with over 17 years of experience in the mortgage industry, consistently driving business growth and development with remarkable success. His deep expertise, strategic vision, and commitment to excellence make him a trusted professional and a valuable asset to the mortgage industry.

Mike Rogozynski

***

One of the things I've always admired about Doug is his focus on looking at ways to create revenue, differentiate his business from the pack, look for supplementary income streams and create a value for his business. In the Canadian mortgage industry, so many broker-owners are too focused on working IN the business to spend the time working ON the business and that's what differentiates Doug from the crowd.

Jason Friesen

***

I am not surprised that Doug has decided to share more of his knowledge with The Business of Brokering. He has always strived to make the industry a better business through his actions, and what better way than through a book.

Brad Knight

***

With The Business of Brokering, Doug Adlam provides a fresh perspective on how our industry can continue to evolve. It's a resource every broker and industry partner should keep close at hand.

Bhavna Bhasin

***

The Business of Brokering is more than a guide — it's a blueprint for building a mortgage business that grows, scales, and creates lasting value. Doug Adlam's experience, dating back to 2008, shines through every page, offering clarity, credibility, and practical strategies that elevate our industry. A must-read for brokers at any stage.

Jessi Johnson

***

I've always admired Doug for the way he's elevated the mortgage profession through both his leadership and his willingness to share what he's learned. His ability to distill complex ideas into practical strategies makes him a valuable voice in our industry. This book is a meaningful resource for brokers looking to build stronger businesses.

Greg Williamson

***

Over the course of my 20-year career in mortgage brokering, Doug's guidance has been invaluable. His insights have shaped the way I approach structuring my team, and he gave me the confidence to do it. It's truly exciting to see his expertise distilled into a book—an exceptional resource that allows others to benefit from the clarity and depth of Doug's strategic thinking provided invaluable mortgage advice to me over my 20 years of brokering. It's amazing to see his advice available in a book for all to reap the rewards of Doug's incredible thought process.

Krista Lindstrom

***

Doug Adlam is a standout mortgage professional and entrepreneur whose expertise and client-first approach set him apart. As the author of The Business of Brokering, he continues to elevate the industry with practical insights and leadership. A true thought leader and trusted advisor.

Reaza Ali

***

I've known Doug for over 15 years and have seen the evolution and the scaling of the brokerage as a tried and true testament to The Business of Brokering and its results.

Ara Manoukian

***

Doug's combination of inspiring leadership, motivational energy, and significant experience in both public speaking and entrepreneurial ventures makes him someone who offers value and thought-provoking insights on a plethora of topics. I've been the beneficiary of his gracious guidance on important opportunities in my career which I'll always be grateful for.

Ruvani Henriques

***

In The Business of Brokering, Doug blends forward-thinking strategy with a grounded, people-first approach that this industry truly needs. His creative insights and commitment to community connection make this book stand out—not just as a guide to brokering, but as a roadmap to building a business with purpose. Doug challenges the status quo and invites mortgage professionals to think bigger, lead boldly, and grow something truly lasting.

Cheryl Buhs

***

Doug Adlam has been a consummate professional and inspirational leader in our industry for many years. His pragmatic approach has served his clients and his lending partners well throughout.

He is a trusted source, and both new & experienced professionals can learn from his experiences.

Frank Giacomini

***

Doug has put together a combination of very insightful and key factors to consider in all aspects of building and maintaining a successful mortgage brokerage, and how to be ready to exit at any time whilst leaving a successful legacy. There is no book out there like it as Doug reveals an extraordinary level of guidance, from firsthand knowledge, that will go a long way for new brokers to experienced brokers to lender partners.

Livia Pellegrino

Foreword

The Canadian mortgage industry is built on relationships, trust, and expertise. Every day, brokers across this country help families realize the dream of homeownership while navigating a marketplace that is constantly changing. To thrive, brokers need more than technical knowledge—they need a roadmap for building sustainable businesses, adapting to new realities, and forging strong partnerships.

The Business of Brokering is exactly that roadmap. It is a book written from a neutral perspective that goes beyond day-to-day sales to address the full lifecycle of a brokerage: how to start, how to grow, and how to prepare for the future. This is a book for every broker, at every stage of their career. This book isn't just a great tool for brokers, it is just as relevant for industry partners who want to better understand the challenges and opportunities that brokers face.

What makes this work especially valuable is its focus on the business side of our profession. Not enough attention has been brought to the fact that brokers are entrepreneurs, and like any entrepreneur they must think about strategy, scale, leadership, and succession. By shining a light on these themes, Doug Adlam has given our industry a resource that will stand the test of time.

At CMLS, we believe in the power of education and partnership. We know that when brokers succeed, the entire mortgage ecosystem becomes stronger. That is why we are proud to support this book and its mission.

Our role as a lender is not only to provide competitive products, but to contribute to the long-term health of the broker channel. This book aligns perfectly with that vision.

Reading these pages, you will find ideas that challenge you, frameworks that guide you, and stories that inspire you. Some chapters will cause you to reflect on your own business, others will spark conversations with your team or partners, and many will give you practical steps you can implement right away.

The mortgage industry has never stood still — and never should; we all know that the pace of change today is greater than ever. With resources like *The Business of Brokering*, we can meet that change with confidence.

To every broker and industry partner holding this book: congratulations on investing in your growth. The insights here will not only help you build better businesses, but also strengthen the fabric of our industry. That is something we can all celebrate.

Andrew Gilmour, CFA
Senior Vice President, Residential
CMLS

Acknowledgements

This book would not have been possible without the support, encouragement, and inspiration of so many people.

First and foremost, my deepest gratitude goes to my family and friends for standing by me through every chapter of this journey.

To all the incredible people I have had the opportunity to work with across every company I've been a part of, my business partners and every single team member, you have shaped my path in countless ways. To the industry leaders who have collaborated with me—lender executives, managers, account managers, underwriters, fulfillment officers, funders, and so many others—thank you for your trust and partnership.

I am especially grateful to my mastermind group, the investors who believed early, and the alpha and beta testers who gave their time and feedback to help bring ideas to life. To every broker and brokerage owner who made time for me in the many roles I've carried throughout my career, I deeply appreciate your openness and insights. To every client I worked with directly or through the incredible teams I had the honour to help lead, thank you for trusting us with such an important part of your lives.

A heartfelt thank you to my industry mentors who invested their time in me, offering wisdom and guidance that shaped both my career and character. To my Entrepreneur's Organization chapters and colleagues who have continued to serve as my personal board of directors, always pushing me to grow as a leader and entrepreneur, I am deeply grateful. To the mortgage industry associations, conferences, and organizations who have given me the opportunity to share my story, and to the audiences who have listened, challenged, and encouraged me along the way—thank you for giving life to the ideas in this book.

I also want to thank the authors who generously shared tips with me, the publishing team who helped bring this book to life, and all those who donated their time to proofread, provide feedback, and contribute endorsements for both the book and myself as an author. Your generosity and belief mean more than I can put into words.

This book is, in many ways, a reflection of all of you.

Introduction

When I entered the mortgage industry in 2008, I didn't have a roadmap. There was no clear structure or a simple "follow these five steps to success" that I could follow. But I wasn't completely lost either. While I didn't have a map, I had spent the previous year designing a business plan down to the details before I ever funded my first deal. It was almost like going on a hike in the mountains without a map, but memorizing the track you'll be walking on beforehand. I had no map, but I had a plan. The year of research and planning seemed excessive to some, but it created the groundwork I needed. It provided me with structure. But no matter how much you prepare, the real education starts when you step onto the field. It happens in conversations with clients, late-night problem-solving sessions, and scaling through seasons of change. No matter how much I planned, there were certain things that could only be learned through experience.

My mortgage journey began at *Champion Mortgage*, the family brokerage my parents built. I always knew that having my parents' brokerage to lean on was a massive blessing and not something to take for granted. But I also wanted to do my own thing and grow beyond my starting point. So, I opened a branch in Guelph, Ontario. Over time, I helped grow that brokerage over 40 times its original size. Along the journey, we won some industry accolades at the Canadian Mortgage Awards for Customer Service (2015) and Brokerage of the Year – under 25 employees (2017 and 2020 Silver). While I experienced significant growth in the mortgage brokerage industry, I still wanted to do more and be more. The desire to do more led me to my next adventure: co-founding Finmo, a mortgage technology company created to simplify and modernize the mortgage experience. What started as an idea born out of conversations about the industry and the gaps we saw, turned into a national platform. It caught the attention of many big industry players and was acquired in 2020 by *Lendesk*. Letting go of Finmo wasn't easy. It was challenging to exit the company we had worked so hard for, but it was also very rewarding to see it thrive.

Shortly before that exit, we moved *Champion Mortgage* to *Axiom*, which we later rebranded to *Indi Mortgage*. We did this to tap into the operational and strategic benefits of a large brokerage. Shortly after the *Finmo* exit, I moved into my first executive leadership role as Director of Strategic Growth at *Indi Mortgage*. It was my job to help lead its transformation from a primarily regional brokerage to a national operation. In just two and a half years, we scaled the business more than fourfold, adding billions in annual mortgage originations. It was during this time that I started to reflect on my journey. I realized that so many of the questions I had, the mistakes I had made, and the growth I had experienced could be helpful to others. A new desire was born: one to help others achieve the same growth I had seen in my own career and mortgage businesses. With this new desire and dream, I stepped down from my director role in early 2024, and just over a year later, I also stepped down from my team leadership role, ready for another new adventure.

That's what led me here: writing this book to help you build, scale, and sell your mortgage business. My new adventure, Adlam Innovations, is different from all the previous adventures I've been on—it's a beautiful accumulation of all my experience. But it's not just a business. I see it as a platform to empower professionals in the mortgage, real estate, and related industries to design a business that's created to be scaled and sold.

Whether through strategy, consulting, research, speaking, or writing a book, the goal is the same: help high-integrity leaders think more clearly and act more intentionally.

Over the years, I've learned that while achieving awards and being recognized in the field is great, the culture and consistency that earned those awards are worth far more. I don't want to teach you how to "win awards." If that happens, great bonus. But I want to help you build something that matters to you. I've experienced many changes in my life. I went from computer Systems Engineer to Market Researcher, to Elite Ice Hockey referee, to Professor, to business innovator, but through it all, I learned valuable lessons I'd like to share.

But don't get me wrong, this book isn't a memoir or a desperate cry for a pat on the back.

It's a playbook. Perhaps even a roadmap.

One I didn't have when I started, but crafted over years and years of ups and downs. A playbook I would now like to pay forward to the next generation of exceptional industry leaders and builders. Whether you're a solo broker chasing your first $30 million year, building a $400 million team, or scaling a multi-billion-dollar brokerage, this book is for you. You'll find frameworks, strategy, stories, and straight talk to help you navigate the choices that matter most in this business. The truth is, this industry rewards those who are intentional builders.

So, let's do just that. Let's build something meaningful and intentional.

Let's build something that can scale and sell.

Let's build something together.

PART ONE
BUILD

Chapter 1

Why Do You Really Want This?

Have you ever dreamt of something for so long that you can't imagine your life without that goal? It's what motivates you. What keeps the midnight oil burning. It's the reason for getting up in the morning and working harder than you thought possible. You know, that goal that consumes you and drives you to push further and further so you can reach it. But what happens when you reach that goal? What happens when you get to the top of the mountain after the intense summit and just have to stop?

Well, in 2016, I reached my peak. Our mortgage business was at an all-time high. We had record profits, clients who were thrilled with our work, and a team that ran like a well-oiled machine. On paper, I had done it. I had reached my goal. I was at the top of the mountain, able to take in the view. I expected the view to take my breath away. I expected to feel a sense of accomplishment and pride. I expected a movie moment where I could finally pat myself on the back and say, "We made it, kid." On paper, I had everything I had ever wanted and worked for.

Yet, I was absolutely miserable.

What I thought would be the best moment of my life felt like my lowest. Instead of taking in the view and relishing in the success, the same question ran through my mind: Why did I do all of this? Why did I want this in the first place? Why did I invest so much of myself into this? Shouldn't I feel better?

As I found myself at the top of my game, I also felt empty. I was burnt out, emotionally depleted, and exhausted beyond what words can describe. I made it, but at what cost? For the first time in my life, I came face to face with a truth that challenged my very being and purpose. I knew that I didn't want to do it anymore. It broke my heart to think about it. It killed me to know that we had built something great, something different, and something remarkable, and that I couldn't take it anymore.

The thought of meeting up with another client felt like walking to the gallows, which was a big wake-up call for me. You see, I consider myself an outgoing person, someone who generally enjoys meeting and interacting with others. But at that stage in my life, I lost that part of myself. The thought of walking anyone through the mortgage journey was crippling. It's almost like I got to the top of the summit only to realize I didn't like the view.

A few weeks later, after this realization, I had a planned meeting with my mastermind group, and it was there that I told them I was shutting it all down. While it was a hard conversation to have, I didn't see any other choice. In my head, there were only two clear paths: go on as I was, or give it all up. But then someone in my mastermind group asked me a valuable question: Why give it up? Why not just delegate?

It was such a simple question, yet one that I didn't even consider. You see, I had worked so hard to build the company and make it a success that I thought I was irreplaceable. Surely the business wouldn't be able to run without me...or would it? The more I thought about it, the more I knew that it was the right call. I realized that I didn't have to sweep away the good with the bad just because I felt done. Perhaps there was another way to make it work—a third path that I hadn't considered initially.

That one simple question saved our business, but it also did so much more than that. It saved me. It reshaped my entire entrepreneurial mindset. Without that one, simple question, I wouldn't be where I am today, with so much more to offer. That question allowed us to regroup as a team, and it pushed me to grow. I handed off every client-facing responsibility, sat back, and waited. Instead of going down the mountain, I pitched a tent and waited for the view to get better. I rested and watched in awe as my business not only survived, but thrived without me. Finally, I found joy in the view. I had my movie moment of awe-filled inspiration and pride. Turns out, it wasn't just the goals that drove me. It wasn't just the thought of success. Instead, it was being able to take it a step further and hand it over.

In that moment, I found my new *why*. Turns out, my why was never just to build. It was to build, scale, and sell. It was the beginning of my evolution from mortgage broker to business owner, and it was spectacular.

Why am I sharing this with you? Because you also need to find your why.

Finding Your Why

Whether you're new to the industry or have been around the block a couple of times, it's never too late to identify your why. So, if no one has ever asked you this before, allow me to be the first: Why are you doing this? Why do you want to be in this industry? Without a why, you'll end up making the same mistakes I did, working toward a goal that's not part of your true desires. Take a moment to consider your why. Don't worry about what your answer *should* be. Be real with yourself. Are you in this industry because you want to build something sellable? Perhaps it's because you want to achieve more freedom of time or maximize your income? Maybe you want to build a legacy or positively impact your community? The good thing is, there are no right or wrong answers here. My goal is not to convince you of some moral code or some cliche quote about never working a day in your life. If you're simply doing this to make money, that's fine by me. Own it.

Why is finding the why so important? Because there's a wrong assumption that success will feel good regardless of your motivation. That's not the case at all. How can you experience success and feel the thrill of achievement when you have never defined what you want to achieve? How can you celebrate success if you don't know what success means to you? Only by identifying your why can you make decisions that will lead you to success that is satisfying. Otherwise, you'll end up with success on paper and still feel empty inside (speaking from experience). Once you identify your why, or call it your purpose, every decision you make, from CRM selection to brokerage structure and branding, should flow from that purpose.

Let's begin this journey on the right foot and allow ourselves to really ask the question of *why*. Remember, this isn't about a nice-sounding answer for the website or for a tagline on your business card. This can be raw, honest, and vulnerable. It's about discovering the true motivation and the fuel that will keep you resilient when things get tough. Here are some simple steps you can follow to find your why right now.

Step 1: List Your Initial Reasons

Start by writing down every reason you can think of for wanting this career and business. When you think of starting or growing your mortgage business, what reasons pop into your mind? Don't overthink it. Write freely and list as many as you can think of. Your list might include financial independence, being your own boss, helping families achieve homeownership, building generational wealth, your love of sales and negotiation.

Step 2: Dig Deeper

Now that you have an initial list with possible "whys," it's time to dig a little deeper. Take each reason and go deeper by using the 5 Whys Method. If you're not familiar, the 5 Whys Method is when you ask yourself why over and over again until you get to the bottom of your real desires and needs. For example, if your reason is to have financial independence, this is what the 5 Whys will look like in action:

- I want financial independence.

- Why? Because I want control over my time.

- Why? Because I want to spend more time with my family.

- Why? Because I missed out on family time growing up.

- Why? Because my parents worked long hours.

- Why? Because they didn't have the opportunity to build a business.

Now your deeper why is not just financial independence, but about creating a better work-life balance and building opportunities that your family never had.

Step 3: Identify What Energizes You

Think back to moments when you've felt most energized or proud, either in or outside of work. Write down what you were doing when you felt like that, who you were helping, and what skills you were using. As you write down these pockets of joy and purpose, try to look for patterns. These moments often reveal your natural strengths and passions, which can be key parts of your purpose.

Step 4: Align Your Values

The next step is to consider your personal values. What principles matter most to you? For example, do you value integrity, service, growth, freedom, creativity, etc.? It's important to know your personal values before you start building something because if you don't, you might end up building a business that clashes with your core values. When that happens, burnout is inevitable.

Step 5: Write Your Statement

Now, let's bring it all together, shall we? It's time to finally consider all the answers and write your statement. "I'm in this business because…" Here are a few examples:

- I am in this business because I want to help families build wealth and stability through homeownership while creating financial freedom for my own family.

- I am in this business because I love solving complex problems and helping clients navigate one of the biggest financial decisions of their lives.

- I am in this business because I believe in building a business that allows me to grow personally, serve others, and create a legacy for my children.

Remember, these are only examples. You should write a statement that is brutally raw and personal to you. That's the only way to truly find your why and hang on to it.

Step 6: Test It

Once you have your statement containing your why, put it to the test. Read it out loud. How does it feel? Does it evoke emotions and motivation? Does it make you proud and inspire you? Could it sustain you through both success and failure? If it doesn't quite feel there yet, go back and refine some of the steps until you find a statement that is deeply personal and motivational to you.

Your purpose isn't set in stone. As your business and your life evolve, you may revisit your why and adjust it accordingly, and that's okay. As long as you never operate without one. When you find your why, all other major decisions will become easier to make. Use it as your compass to guide you on the path of building, evolving, and eventually exiting. I will forever be grateful for asking myself why I felt so empty when I was supposed to be overjoyed. I will also be forever grateful to my crew for asking me why I wanted to give up the business rather than delegate. Without those two questions, I would never have found my real purpose and why, which is this: helping others along the same path in the business of brokering.

So, don't underestimate your why. It will carry you through. It will guide you and cheer you on. It will form you and help you to evolve into the person you want to be. It will make every summit worth the blood, sweat, and tears. More importantly, it will make success feel like success, both on paper and within yourself.

Free Download: Finding Your Why Worksheet

For a free downloadable worksheet to help you clarify your "why" and align it with your business goals, go to: dougadlam.com/brokering

Or scan the QR code below:

Chapter 2

Startup Strong—Incorporation, Protection, and Agreements

Let's be real for a second: The why you just determined for getting into the mortgage business probably doesn't include the tagline "Because I'm passionate about corporate structures, insurance policies, and contract clauses." It's more personal and motivating than that, I would hope. So, why then immediately jump from the importance of finding your why to...this?

Let me put it this way: Imagine you're a kid who dreams of making it to the big leagues—the PWHL or NHL. You can already see yourself out there under the lights, standing on the blue line during the national anthem, the crowd buzzing with energy. You can hear the roar as the puck drops at center ice. The dream feels so real you can almost touch it. But how do you get there?

You start with the basics: getting your first pair of skates. You wobble across the rink, learning how to stay upright. Then comes your first stick, your first puck, and those early morning practices at hockey school where you learn to skate and stickhandle at the same time. After that, you join your first team, play your first game, and begin to understand what it means to work hard, show up, and play as part of something bigger. Every pass, every shift, every practice is a step toward that dream.

And just like in hockey, building something meaningful—whether it's a career, a business, or a leadership legacy—starts with mastering the fundamentals and taking intentional steps forward, one stride at a time.

Now, let's apply that same principle to your mortgage business. You have your why. You are fueled with inspiration and motivation, and you know what success will look like. But we can't skip ahead. We need to focus on building a solid foundation to ensure the outcome is everything you aspire for it to be. These three elements are what create a strong startup and what will catapult you toward success: Incorporation, Protection, and Agreements. Are these elements the most exciting part of building a business? Not even close. But are they absolutely vital? Yes. This is where it all begins.

Whether you're starting a new business or have already been running one for years, it's never too late to clean up and restructure the foundation. These three elements will help you to grow, protect, and ultimately sell your mortgage business, so don't underestimate their importance. Let's break it down and explore why each of these elements is so crucial and how you can build them into your foundation.

Incorporation: More Than a Tax Move

Incorporation isn't just about saving on taxes. It's about protecting your personal assets and creating a legitimate, transferable entity. Incorporating signals to others and yourself that you're building something bigger than a job. You're building something real. Something with value. But what exactly is incorporation? Incorporation is the legal process of creating a separate business entity, typically a corporation, that exists independently from you as an individual. When you incorporate, your business becomes its own legal "person" in the eyes of the law. It can own property, enter into contracts, hire employees, pay taxes, and even borrow money.

In Canada, you can incorporate federally or provincially, depending on where you plan to operate. Each option has its own advantages, but both achieve the same core purpose: They separate your personal life from your business life. But why go through the effort of incorporating? Is it really that beneficial? Yes, and here's why.

Legal Separation Between Personal and Business Liabilities

As I just mentioned, when you incorporate, your business becomes a separate legal entity. This creates a protective barrier between your personal assets and your business activities. So, hypothetically, if your company faces legal action, debt, or financial loss for some reason, all your personal assets will be safe. That includes your home, savings, vehicles, and investments. Now, of course, we never start a business with the belief that it will fail or run into trouble, but it's still good to have that barrier of protection, even when the risks are low. This limited liability structure gives you peace of mind as you take on clients, hire staff, and navigate the inevitable risks of running a business. As always, consult with your trusted lawyer to understand the benefits and risks associated with your situation. Please note that I am not providing any legal advice here.

More Flexibility With Income Splitting and Reinvestment

Incorporation opens up powerful tax planning tools that aren't available to sole proprietors. As a corporation, you have more control over various elements, including how and when you pay yourself. This means you can choose whether you want to pull a salary, dividends, or a combination. It also presents income splitting opportunities, where you can pay dividends to others involved in the business. Lastly, incorporation means retaining profits within the corporation, as it allows you to defer personal income tax and use those funds to reinvest in business growth, marketing, staffing, or expansion initiatives. This flexibility becomes especially valuable as your business scales, your personal income grows, and your financial planning becomes more sophisticated.

Opening the Door to Future Valuation and Sale

Incorporating your business lays the groundwork for future business valuation and potential sale. A properly structured corporation is easier to value because it stands apart from you personally. This makes your mortgage business more attractive to future buyers, partners, or investors who want to acquire an established entity with clear financials, transferable assets, and existing contracts. Whether your long-term goal is retirement, succession, or exit, incorporation gives you options and leverage when that time comes.

My pro tip is to incorporate before you scale. That way, it's easier and much cheaper. The earlier you do it in the process, the more beneficial it will be later on.

Insurance: Protecting the Business and the Builder

Insurance is the seatbelt of entrepreneurship. Like wearing a seatbelt, taking out insurance might not always feel like the most urgent thing. It's the beginning phase of a business; what could go wrong, right? Well, everything! Insurance doesn't feel urgent until it's the only thing that saves you. When you're building a mortgage business, it's easy to focus on growth: clients, commissions, team building, and lead generation. But here's the thing: none of it matters if one unexpected event wipes it all out. A lawsuit, a disability, a sudden illness—these aren't just possibilities, they're realities many professionals face at some point in their careers.

It's not always exciting and motivating to think of all the things that could go wrong. It's more comfortable to assume that these bad things only happen to others, but this isn't the time to bury your head in the sand like an ostrich. If your income, reputation, or operations suffer a hit and you're unprotected, you risk losing more than just a month's commission. You risk your entire business and everything you've worked so hard to build. But this isn't about living and operating a business from a place of fear. It's about being smart. It's about creating a baseline

THE BUSINESS OF BROKERING

of protection that allows your business to thrive with confidence. Let's look at the key types of insurance every Canadian mortgage professional should seriously consider.

Errors and Omissions (E&O) Insurance

This is non-negotiable. As a licensed mortgage professional, E&O insurance is required by your regulator. It protects you against claims of negligence, errors in advice, or failure to act. Now, here's the thing. You and I know that your intention will never be to lead someone astray. However, even with the best intentions and practices, mistakes can still occur. No matter who you are, you're not perfect. Don't make the mistake of thinking you're above these kinds of mistakes because you have good intentions. It's not enough. You need to be prepared because lawsuits can be financially devastating. Errors and Omissions Insurance covers legal defense costs, settlements or judgments, and maintains your professional credibility and continuity of operations.

Commercial General Liability (CGL) Insurance

If you have a physical office, staff, or host client-facing meetings or events, you need CGL insurance. This protects your business from claims related to bodily injury, property damage, and advertising liability. Remember, one slip on your office floor can cause a whole avalanche of consequences. Cover yourself, your business, and your stakeholders with CGL insurance and avoid getting into situations you'd rather not be in. CGL is particularly important if you operate out of a co-working space or leased office, if you run seminars, workshops, or networking events, or if you employ admin or support staff who interact with clients. Even if you primarily work from home, consider this a small cost to cover the "what-ifs."

Key Person Insurance

If your business relies primarily on you (your name, your relationships, your ability to bring in revenue), then *you* are a key asset. Key Person Insurance protects the business itself if something happens to you. This is typically a life insurance or disability policy owned by the corporation. If you pass away or become disabled, the business receives a payout that can be used to cover lost revenue, pay off business debts, or fund a temporary replacement or transition plan. This kind of coverage helps ensure the business survives long enough to be sold, restructured, or stabilized.

Disability and Critical Illness Insurance

Here's a little reality check for you: If your entire income stream depends on your ability to show up, make calls, and close deals, one accident or illness could mean zero revenue. That's not business. That's a job with a massive risk attached to it. Personal disability insurance and critical illness coverage protect your ability to earn income and continue building equity in your business, even if you can't work for a period of time. The payout can help cover personal and business expenses, reduce the need to sell assets or take on debt, and maintain your long-term goals, even during recovery. If you're planning to scale your business, grow a team, or sell it all one day, this kind of protection is what separates the professionals from the exposed.

I want to encourage you to view insurance as a foundation for your business, not an afterthought. Later in the book, we'll revisit insurance and explore risk management, business valuation, and preparing your company for sale, but for now, all you need to consider is the baseline protection. You wouldn't build a house without insurance, right? So, don't build your business without it either.

Agreements: Read Them, Understand Them, Revisit Them

So many brokers sign onto a brokerage or network without thoroughly reading their contracts. I've seen it time and time again: Someone builds a strong book of business over several years, decides it's time to move on, and then gets blindsided by non-solicits, clawbacks, and restrictions they didn't even know they had agreed to. It's heartbreaking, devastating, and avoidable. Contracts aren't just paperwork. They are the rulebook that governs your rights, restrictions, and future options. If you're building a business, you no longer have the luxury of skipping over the small print and the terms and conditions pages. You must read everything carefully and ensure you understand what you're reading.

The terms you sign today will shape the value and freedom of your business tomorrow. If you wouldn't let a client sign a mortgage commitment without understanding it, don't do it with your business agreements either. Here are some key agreements every mortgage professional should review, understand, and maintain from the start.

Incorporation Document and Shareholder Agreements

If you've incorporated your business, as we covered earlier, your Articles of Incorporation and Shareholder Agreement form the legal backbone of your company. These documents outline who owns what percentage of the company, including voting rights and decision-making powers, how profits are distributed, and what will happen if a shareholder wishes to exit, passes away, or becomes incapacitated. If you're a solo owner, this might seem like overkill, but if you ever plan to bring on a partner, a team member with equity, or outside investors, having a clear stakeholder agreement in place will help avoid massive future headaches and protect the business you're building.

Employment and Contractor Agreements With Your Team

As your business grows, you'll likely bring on help. This might be assistants, underwriters, business development reps, or even additional brokers. Whether they're full-time employees or independent contractors, you must put agreements in writing. These contracts should clearly define the roles and responsibilities, compensation and bonuses, termination clauses, confidentiality and non-solicitation terms, as well as ownership of leads, contacts, and intellectual property. Clarity here prevents misaligned expectations, protects your client database, and ensures that if someone leaves, they don't take your systems or your pipeline with them.

Your Brokerage or Network Agreement

This is a huge one. Whether you're joining a national brand or a boutique shop, your brokerage and/or network agreement can contain critical restrictions you'll want to fully understand before you sign…not after. Here are some things to look out for:

- Clawback clauses, which state that you may have to repay commissions if a deal is paid out within a certain time period, are often in line with lender policies.

- Non-compete or non-solicitation terms, which might state that you can or cannot contact your own clients if you leave.

- Ownership of leads, stating who the leads belong to (personal or brokerage).

- Portability of your book, stating whether you can take your database and branding with you.

- Whether your split/fee can change without notice or is guaranteed not to change over a predefined time period.

- With most brokers laser-focused on split, what other aspects of the agreement have fees that could change at any time.

It's so important to read everything line by line. And if something doesn't make sense, get legal advice. The fine print could determine whether you control your career or end up locked in a golden cage. My pro tip is to revisit these agreements periodically. Business isn't static, and neither are contracts. As you scale, bring on partners, or shift brokerages, your rights and responsibilities will evolve. Make it a habit to review your key agreements at least once a year. Things change. A restriction that didn't matter a few years ago might become a limitation when you're running a team. Don't let buried clauses catch you off guard.

Agreement of Understanding

One of the most underutilized yet powerful tools in a mortgage broker's toolkit isn't a marketing strategy or a rate special, but a clear, professional Agreement of Understanding. While mortgage regulations differ by province, most restrict brokers from charging upfront or cancellation fees unless very specific, regulated conditions are met. Still, many brokers attempt to protect their time and energy by crafting informal "consultation fees" or threatening cancellation penalties, often without enforceability or clarity. The result? Confusion, frustration, and a client experience that lacks professionalism.

When I first introduced an Agreement of Understanding into our process, the goal wasn't to bind clients legally. It wasn't about locking people in. It was about aligning expectations early. The agreement served as a mutual commitment: The client was choosing to work with our brokerage exclusively throughout the mortgage process, and we were committing to serve them with diligence, strategy, and care. It outlined what that relationship looked like, including expectations if the client disengaged after significant work had already been done.

For those with a background in real estate, this might sound familiar. Realtors have long used buyer representation agreements or listing contracts to formally define their relationship with clients. It's a standard, even expected, part of doing business. And yet, in the mortgage space, we often shy away from formal structure in the name of flexibility. But that flexibility can cost us: in time, in reputation, in compensation, and in lender relationships. It also costs the mortgage ecosystem, ultimately resulting in higher mortgage rates for Canadians.

Introducing this document into our process brought clarity and confidence. Clients appreciated the transparency. Our team felt more secure knowing that the groundwork for a professional partnership had been clearly laid. And lenders responded positively too: We experienced less churn, fewer pulled deals, and better alignment throughout the approval process.

A key component of our agreement was clarity around when clients could shop. We made it clear that clients were welcome, encouraged even, to do their research, ask questions, and decide who they wanted to work with. But once a mortgage application was submitted on their behalf to a lender, that submission represented a mutual commitment to move forward with the process.

Think about how this plays out in real estate: Once a buyer submits an offer through a realtor and it's accepted, they don't then switch agents at the eleventh hour because someone else offers them a lower commission or cash. That would be unethical and professionally unacceptable. Yet in our industry, these last-minute switches happen all too often, undermining the integrity of the process and devaluing the work brokers put in behind the scenes. The Agreement of Understanding helps shift that culture. It sets a professional tone, reduces ambiguity, and protects both the client and the broker. It's not about being rigid; it's about creating shared accountability.

This agreement doesn't just help you; it also helps your lenders. When fewer deals fall apart at the last minute, lenders can operate more efficiently, allocate their underwriting resources more effectively, and improve their service levels, all of which benefits your clients and your brand. So, whether you're a solo broker or building a national team, consider creating your own version of this agreement, tailored to your provincial regulations and business model. It's not just a tool for protection but one that should reflect how seriously you take your work.

You'll hear more about agreements and other documents throughout this book, especially when we start talking about partnerships, aggregation, and making your business attractive to buyers. But here's the mindset shift to start with: A great agreement protects everyone. A vague or one-sided one puts your future at risk. You don't need to enroll in law classes to understand everything, but you do need to care. Every signature you make is a strategic decision.

That wraps up the three foundational pillars of a strong startup: Incorporation, Insurance, and Agreements. Together, they turn your hustle into business and your business into an asset. When your foundation is solid, you'll make decisions faster, delegate with confidence, and grow without fear.

So, build it once, and build it right.

Free Download: Contract Review Checklist

For a free downloadable checklist to help you review agreements with confidence and avoid common pitfalls, go to:
dougadlam.com/brokering

Or scan the QR code below:

Chapter 3

Choosing the Right Network and Brokerage

With your why in place and your foundation built, the next major decision to make on your journey is choosing the right network and brokerage. The decision to align with a particular brokerage or network is one of the most important, and probably the most defining, choices you'll make in your mortgage career. It influences everything. Compensation, structure, technological tools, marketing reach, and even the long-term value of your business will largely be influenced by the network and brokerage you choose.

Unfortunately, this is also a decision that's not very straightforward. This is an industry that's fast-paced and relationship-driven, which adds additional complexities to this decision. It's very tempting to chase the shiniest offer with higher splits, bigger volume bonuses, slick marketing packages, and upfront signing incentives. But those offers aren't necessarily the best ones for you. While they might sweeten the short-term experience, it's vital to know this one truth: Value and alignment will always beat flashy in the long run.

What you really need is a brokerage or network that fits you. That includes your stage of growth, your working style, your ambitions, and your appetite for support versus independence. The right environment can accelerate your success, give you leverage, and create stability, which are all worth a lot more than an immediate signing bonus. The wrong environment can hold you back, box you in, and create friction where you should be building momentum.

That's why this chapter is dedicated to helping you make a clear, strategic decision about where to plant your business. We'll look at how to assess what kind of support and structure you actually need, the pros and cons of joining a network versus going independent, and what to consider when deciding whether to start your own brokerage or join an existing one. While these decisions might feel overwhelming, remember that you don't just want a place to work. You want a platform that amplifies what you do best, aligns with your values (and your why), and gives your business room to evolve. Let's explore how to find it together.

Defining What You Need

I often see brokers who don't know what they need until they need it. This industry is vast and complex, making it difficult to know what the best option is without spending some serious time researching. But before you jump straight in and begin comparing brokerage splits, lead gen tools, or the size of the welcoming package, take a step back. The right brokerage or network is not just about what *they* offer, but about what *you* need. At the end of the day, this is your business. Your name, your reputation, your income. Aligning with the wrong model might be fine in the short term, but it can create friction, frustration, and even lost opportunities down the line. The only way to avoid that is to get radically honest with yourself before you sign anything. So, let's do that right now. Here are three hard, strategic questions you should ask yourself.

Do You Want More Autonomy or More Support?

Some brokers thrive in high-autonomy environments. They want the freedom to choose their tech stack, design their client experience, and make quick decisions without seeking approval. Others prefer the structure, mentorship, and scaffolding of a more hands-on organization that offers training, tools, admin help, and leadership guidance. Neither is right nor wrong, they're just different. Knowing your preference will help you to filter out poor fits quickly. Are you building a one-person empire or hoping to plug into a high-performance system? Take some time to think about it and measure it against your values and your why to ensure that you're choosing the option that will best work for you.

What Kind of Brand Are You Building?

This is a very important question to ask yourself. Are you trying to grow under your personal name and reputation? Or do you want to create a new brand entirely that's bigger than you alone? Maybe it's neither. Maybe you want to leverage an established brokerage brand with proven credibility and reach? Each of these paths has its trade-offs. Building your own brand will give you long-term control and potential asset value, but it will require more investment and consistency. Aligning with a strong brand can lend instant trust and polish, but you may be tied to their messaging, style, and rules. Think about where you want your name to sit in the market. Do you want to be front and center? Or do you want to work quietly behind the scenes? Maybe your sweet spot is somewhere in the middle? Again, none of these answers are correct or incorrect, but you need to have clarity before making a decision.

Are You Comfortable Managing Compliance and Regulatory Risk?

Compliance isn't the sexy part of the business, but it is absolutely critical. If you're considering launching your own franchise brokerage or going fully independent, understand that you're also taking on the responsibility of staying on top of regulatory audits, file reviews, privacy policies, record keeping, anti-money laundering processes, knowing your client requirements, complaint handling, and ongoing license management and training. If that kind of operational oversight energizes you, or if you're planning to hire support to handle it, great. But if the idea of dealing with regulators makes your palms sweat, you might prefer a network or brokerage that shields you from those tasks and has established systems in place.

Taking time to define what you actually need will make your decision process faster, smarter, and more aligned. You'll be able to ignore the noise and focus on what matters most, which is whether the brokerage or network you're considering will truly fit the business you're building (not just today, but in three, five, and ten years down the road).

Network vs. Independent

Once you've clarified your needs around autonomy, support, and brand vision, it's time to explore the five primary brokerage models available in the Canadian mortgage industry. While no model is perfect, understanding how each works will help you align your goals with the structure that best supports your growth.

Fully Independent Brokerages

This model is for those who want full control: no umbrella, no affiliation, just your own name and your own rules. You build the brand, define the client experience, select the tech stack, manage compliance, and hire the team. You're also fully responsible for audits, training, recruitment, marketing, and direct interaction with regulators. The pros? You have total autonomy and full ownership. You shape everything, from the culture to the compensation model. There's no cap on how you scale or sell, and you keep 100% of the revenue and equity you generate. The cons? The flip side is total responsibility. There's no built-in support, mentorship, or operational infrastructure unless you build it yourself or outsource it. The administrative burden and compliance obligations are significant, and it can feel isolating without a strong external network.

This model suits seasoned brokers with a strong pipeline, a clear vision, and the appetite and resources to build something from the ground up.

Independent With Network Affiliation

Think of this as a hybrid: You still create and operate under your own brand, but you plug into a national network for support. In exchange for a monthly fee or a percentage of your sales revenue, you get access to a variety of services, which may include centralized compliance support, technology, training, recognition programs, and often peer communities. The pros? You retain your brand identity and core independence, but with a safety net. This model eases the operational load, provides community and mentorship, and gives you access to tools and services that would be expensive or difficult to implement on your own.

The cons? You'll pay for the support, and often still be subject to network-level expectations or policy changes. Some systems or service providers may be required, and while your business is independent, the network's decisions can still impact your operations. This model works well for brokers who want to grow without recreating the wheel and who value community, shared learning, and scalability without full isolation.

Franchise Brokerages

Franchise models provide the structure of a national brand with the flexibility of local ownership. You operate your business under a franchised name, often one owned by a larger network, and gain access to brand equity, marketing support, compliance systems, and recruiting tools. The pros? Instant consumer trust and credibility. Shared systems and national marketing help drive traffic and reduce your operational burden. You can still build a team and craft a unique experience within the franchise framework.

The cons? You'll pay a percentage of sales or fixed franchise fees. You also face branding and systems restrictions. While you can scale within the model, your flexibility is narrower, and your brand is ultimately tied to the franchise's identity. Franchises are ideal for brokers who want structure, name recognition, and tools but who are also ready to take on leadership and management responsibilities within a more defined framework.

National Brokerages

These brokerages are usually owned by national networks, are members of a network, or, less commonly, operate independently on a national scale. They offer a more turn-key experience where much of the administrative and compliance load is handled for you, allowing you to focus on production. The pros? High-level support, training, mentorship, and access to resources you don't have to build yourself. Often, you'll benefit from enhanced compensation tiers tied to the brokerage's total volume. You'll also be part of a larger team environment with built-in collaboration and systems.

The cons? Less autonomy over your brand, processes, and operations. There's usually little to no opportunity for custom branding or differentiated client experience. Long-term, equity creation may be limited since you're building within someone else's system. This model is a great fit for newer brokers who want to get up and running fast, or for experienced brokers who want to stay in production without the additional burden of brokerage-level responsibilities.

Sub-Brokerage Models

To add another layer of complexity, many of the models above may offer a sub-brokerage or "Team" model. In this setup, you operate under the umbrella of a larger brokerage, but often with your own brand (or a co-branded identity) and a degree of internal control, often over your compensation plan, team structure, and internal systems. The pros? You gain access to the parent brokerage's support systems while building your own branded presence. It's a flexible way to scale a team or leadership model without having to fully branch out on your own.

The cons? Sub-brokerages may not always be recognized at the lender level for volume bonuses or status, and this can impact compensation and leverage. Also, while a sub-brokerage is more protected than a simple "team brand," regulations around team branding can change, and you'll need to stay informed about provincial compliance. The sub-brokerage model can be a powerful stepping stone or a long-term home, depending on your goals.

Here's a bit of a reality check: There's no such thing as a perfect model. Every model comes with trade-offs. Independence can give you full control, but it also means full responsibility. Franchise models offer a mix of freedom and brand power, but they come with fees and limitations. National brokerages can supercharge your start, but might constrain your ability to scale your way. So, don't just ask, "Which model is the best?" Ask, "Which models align best with my goals, risk tolerance, and working style?"

Starting a Brokerage

Starting a brokerage, whether fully independent or as part of a franchise, can seem like the ultimate career milestone. The freedom, the control, the ability to shape your own systems and culture—it's a powerful vision. But like many entrepreneurial pursuits, the dream often looks cleaner on paper than it feels in reality. One of the most common and persistent misconceptions is that starting a brokerage automatically leads to greater financial gain. It's easy to assume that cutting out the middleman will mean keeping more of the pie. After all, you're the owner. Shouldn't more of the revenue land in your pocket? In theory, yes. In practice, it's far more complicated.

Owning a brokerage isn't just about higher compensation. It's about higher responsibility. You're no longer just a producer. You're also an operator, a recruiter, a brand builder, a compliance officer, a culture creator, and so much more. The best way to describe this is by looking at the example of going on a vacation abroad. You can pay more to join an already planned tour group, where you basically just have to show up and participate in the activities outlined in the itinerary. Or, you can plan your own trip, go through all the effort of bargain hunting, booking activities, and cooking food, allowing you to enjoy more control. If you choose the latter, and you are building your brokerage, every piece of the machine belongs to you, and that machine needs fuel in the form of time, money, energy, and leadership. So, here are a few things to consider before choosing this route.

The Motivation to Go Solo

For many brokers, the motivation to start a brokerage isn't just about money. It's often a desire to do things differently. To build a service model that feels more modern, more client-focused, and more aligned with their values. Maybe they've worked inside systems that felt limiting, and they want the freedom to innovate, experiment, and lead. That motivation is valid and powerful.

In my own case, I was fortunate to step into a leadership role within our family's brokerage. I had the autonomy to run my own branch, but with the benefit of shared infrastructure (compliance, underwriting, payroll, technology) already in place. That support made the transition manageable. But not everyone has that advantage. And for many who pursue full independence, the learning curve can be steep and humbling.

The Illusion of Differentiation

One of the first realizations new brokerage owners face is that "doing it differently" is much harder than it sounds. Many enter the market convinced they've discovered a unique approach—a new value proposition that no one else is offering. However, after conducting market research, speaking with other owners, and examining the competitive landscape more closely, they often discover that their model isn't as unique as they initially thought. The truth is, most "new ideas" have already been tried—sometimes multiple times.

True differentiation is hard. It requires more than a clever slogan or fresh logo. It's about consistently delivering a client experience that stands out and being willing to back that up with process, culture, and execution. That takes time, clarity, and capital. Don't fall into the trap of thinking your new idea will immediately take off and take over the industry. It might, but it might also not.

Branding Isn't a Shortcut

This is another myth that's often paired with starting your own brokerage. Believing that if you build a new brand, clients will automatically come is a myth that needs to be busted. It's a seductive idea. A sleek name, a sharp website, a few Instagram posts, and suddenly, you're the next big thing. But branding is not the same as having a brand. Branding is a combination of design and reputation. And reputations don't launch—they accumulate. It's built over time and through client results, market visibility, and consistent delivery. You can invest tens of thousands into branding, but if your system, experience, or leadership don't deliver, it won't matter. Brand equity is earned, not purchased.

Compensation Isn't What It Seems

Even brokers who understand branding and operations often underestimate the financial side. Specifically, they assume they'll be able to recreate the volume bonuses, tiered commissions, and lender perks they enjoyed while under a larger brokerage's umbrella. But many of those perks are tied to your own brokerage volume, not just network performance.

As a new brokerage owner, you're likely starting from scratch with lenders, and it takes sustained, often significant, volume to unlock higher compensation tiers, efficiencies, or elite status. Until you get there, you may be earning less than before, even while working more. This can be especially jarring if you're trying to hire or recruit new talent. Your compensation model may not be as competitive as the one you just left, at least, not in the early stages.

Regulatory Complexity and Cost

Starting a brokerage means stepping into full regulatory responsibility. This means you're in charge of:

- Licensing and renewals

- Anti-money laundering (AML) policies

- Fraud prevention

- File reviews and audit preparedness

- Broker of record duties

- Record retention and privacy protocols

And these are just the baseline. Brokerage-level insurance can also be costly, especially if you're doing private deals. Many brokers don't realize that private lending increases liability, which in turn raises your premiums, and in turn the premiums you are paying for your employees, and the premiums paid by the independent brokers on your team. These costs can quickly add up and eat into early profitability.

Lender Access Isn't Guaranteed

Finally, don't assume your personal relationships with lenders will automatically carry over when you launch a new entity. Some lenders have strict onboarding processes for new brokerages, and they may delay or deny approval, regardless of your track record. Others may place temporary product access caps or restrictions while you build a history under the new license. Are you used to dedicated underwriting support with a rockstar underwriter? You may start back in a pool of underwriters or with a more junior underwriter, even with your top lender. In short, expect a reset of your lender relationship. You'll need to prove yourself all over again.

Am I sharing all of this to convince you not to start your own brokerage? Not at all. I'm simply sharing this with you because I want you to succeed. Being left in the dark or going into something this significant without clarity won't contribute toward a better future; it will hinder it. There's nothing wrong with dreaming of independence, and owning your own brokerage can be deeply fulfilling, as I have experienced myself. But it's not a shortcut to success. It's a long-game commitment that demands clarity, resilience, capital, and leadership. If you do choose this path, do it with your eyes wide open.

Joining a Brokerage

Not every broker dreams of building an independent business from scratch, and that's a good thing. Joining an established brokerage can offer tremendous value, especially if you're early in your career or focused on production rather than operations. But it's not a decision to make lightly. As we have already discussed, too many brokers choose based on superficial perks: higher splits, signing bonuses, and branded technology. But the right brokerage is more than a compensation plan; it's an ecosystem that shapes your business trajectory. The best ones elevate your reputation, support your growth, and free up your time to do what you do best: serve clients and drive deals. Let's break down what to look for and what to watch out for.

Aligning on Philosophy and Vision

Choosing a brokerage isn't just a financial decision; it's a cultural one. You're stepping into someone else's structure, values, and way of doing business. If those things don't match your own, friction is inevitable. So, ask the following questions:

- Does the leadership share my long-term view?

- Are they forward-thinking or just maintaining the status quo?

- Do they invest in systems, innovation, and education, or are they coasting on old wins?

- Is the brokerage built to grow with me, or will I eventually outgrow it?

- Do I want to build something within this structure, or will I constantly be building despite it?

There's nothing more exhausting than trying to grow your business inside a system that resists change. You're not just plugging into a payroll system, but joining a team, a brand, and a reputation. Ensure it fits before making a commitment.

How to Evaluate Signing Incentives

Here's where things can get tricky. Many brokerages and networks offer attractive signing packages that could include upfront cash bonuses, enhanced splits, volume incentives, and proprietary software tools. These are meant to entice, and they often work. But read the fine print. High rewards often, but not always, come with high restrictions. Ask yourself:

- Is there a multi-year commitment?

- Are there clawbacks or repayment clauses if I leave early?

- Does the agreement include a non-solicit, preventing me from bringing my team or clients with me later?

- Will I lose deferred commissions if I exit before a certain date?

- What if the required software doesn't meet my expectations?

- What happens if the brokerage doesn't hit the required volume bonus or efficiency levels?

- Do I maintain ownership and access to my website URL?

- What options do I have if the support doesn't match the promises made?

- Did I run this contract by a lawyer or an industry expert to identify any areas of concern?

If these answers don't align with your values, pause. Even if you trust leadership, remember that people can change and companies will evolve. What seems aligned today could feel restrictive tomorrow. The only thing that will remain is the contract, so make sure it works for you and your long-term goals before signing anything.

A quick pro tip to remember: If it seems too generous on paper, it's probably not in your favour long term.

The People Beside You Matter

In this business, your reputation is a major part of your brand. And when you join a brokerage, you're tying your brand to theirs (and to everyone else under the same banner). That means that their wins will reflect on you, but so will their mistakes, their ethics, their standards, and their practices. So, take a look around and ask yourself: "If I were associated with this particular broker or team under the same logo, would that be bad, good, or great for my business?"

If the answer is bad, walk away. If the answer is good, that's worth exploring. If the answer is great, you've found an edge most brokers never realized they needed. Brand association is real. Perception is powerful. And once you join, you don't get to pick who people assume you're aligned with.

Doing Your Homework

Finally, and this is where many people drop the ball, do your due diligence. Don't rely on a sales pitch from the brokerage's recruiter or owner. They're there to sell. You need unfiltered information. Ask to speak confidently with a top producer or someone who's scaled inside this brokerage, and a similar producer who is ideally someone with a business model like yours. These conversations will tell you more than any presentation ever could. You'll hear what works, what doesn't, and what support actually shows up once the ink is dry. You'll also learn how easy it is to access leadership, whether compliance is responsive or rigid, and if the compensation and marketing promises actually hold up over time.

This is *your* business. Do the kind of due diligence you'd expect your clients to do before signing a mortgage. The brokerage you choose today could be your brand, your earnings, and your exit options for years to come. Treat the decision with the weight it deserves.

Reputation is Everything

Whether you choose to join a brokerage or build your own, one truth holds steady across this entire industry: Your reputation is your greatest asset. It's not just about how you show up; it's about who you choose to stand beside. Your brand is shared real estate. Once you attach your name to a brokerage, network, or franchise, you inherit part of its reputation, whether it's good, bad, or mixed. And just as importantly, your actions impact everyone else carrying that same logo. Reputation doesn't just affect client referrals or Google reviews. It shapes:

- How lenders treat you, both during deals and in volume negotiations

- How top talent responds to your recruiting efforts

- What your business is worth if you ever want to sell

- How your team feels showing up under your banner every day

This industry is smaller than it looks. People talk, word travels, and your reputation will often walk into the room long before you do. Choose wisely. Brand wisely. Partner wisely. If there's one truth that every mortgage professional learns sooner or later, it's this: The business is always changing.

No matter how solid the model you create or how aligned the brokerage (or the network) you join seems today, you should expect and plan for change. Incentive structures evolve. Volume bonuses might shift from being based on personal production to brokerage-wide or even network-level metrics. Tomorrow's performance benchmarks could prioritize efficiency, client retention, or even innovative markers like total client touchpoints.

Networks and brokerages will add or remove services. Leadership teams and ownership structures will change, bringing with them new philosophies and priorities. Regulatory shifts might require brokers to renegotiate contracts, rethink licensing arrangements, or even reconsider their affiliations altogether. A technology stack that's optional today may be mandatory tomorrow, or vice versa, impacting workflows and team adoption. All of this is normal. Change isn't a disruption in this industry; it's part of the rhythm.

That's why flexibility is just as important as alignment. The brokers who thrive aren't the ones clinging to a single model but the ones who stay adaptable, remain strategic, and build businesses that can evolve as the market does. Choose your current environment wisely, yes, but more importantly, stay engaged, stay informed, and be willing to recalibrate when necessary. In a shifting landscape, your ability to pivot is a powerful competitive advantage.

Free Download: Needs Analysis Worksheet

For a free downloadable worksheet to identify your priorities and determine where you need support, go to: dougadlam.com/brokering

Or scan the QR code below:

Chapter 4

Tech Decisions That Make
or Break Your Business

Technology can be a defining factor in whether your mortgage business scales or stalls. In many ways, your tech decisions are almost as important as choosing the right network and brokerage. While technology can be utilized in various ways within your organization, there are two categories that we need to focus on more: Customer Relationship Management Systems and Deal Management Systems. While many brokers treat Customer Relationship Management systems (CRM) and Deal Management Systems (DMS) as background tools or necessary evils, the truth is, they're the infrastructure of your business. They shape your client experience, your operational efficiency, your compliance practices, and your ability to delegate, grow, or sell down the road.

If you ignore CRM and DMS, you're choosing to fly blind, and if you choose the wrong ones, you end up wasting your time, losing clients, and frustrating your team. So, what can we do? We need to focus on making strategic, sellable tech decisions, not just for where you are now, but for where you're going. In this chapter, we'll unpack the difference between CRM and DMS, look at what features matter, and how industry politics, integrations, and ownership dynamics can (and should) influence your choices when it comes to tech.

Whether you're currently a solo broker looking to streamline follow-up or a growing team aiming to automate workflows, your tech stack needs to support your future goals, not just your current workload. Because when it comes to this business, how you manage information is how you manage relationships, and how you manage relationships is how you win. Let's get right to it.

CRM vs. DMS

First, let's get crystal clear on the distinction between these two core systems that are often confused, or worse, lumped together as interchangeable.

Your CRM (Customer Relationship Management) is your relationship engine. It's where your contact data lives, your communication history is logged, and your client lifecycle is tracked, from first contact to post-closing and beyond. A well-built CRM helps you to:

- Automate follow-ups and nurture campaigns

- Track client anniversaries, renewal dates, and referral opportunities

- Segment your database for targeted marketing

- Stay top-of-mind without being spammy

- Build predictable referral pipelines over time

- Oversee marketing, sales, and operational performance

In other words, it's your system for staying human at scale. Remembering birthdays, following up after funding, and showing up consistently are musts if you want to remain relational as you grow your company.

Your DMS (Deal Management System), on the other hand, is the operational core of your mortgage business. It's where you build, manage, and submit live mortgage files. It handles:

- Document collection and compliance workflows

- Lender submissions and status tracking

- Client portals for application input

- Task management and brokerage audit trails

- Broker-lender communications and notes

The DMS ensures that your files are funded, stay compliant, and don't fall through the cracks. Both of these systems are crucial, but they don't accomplish the same goal. However, in the Canadian mortgage industry, you'll find some platforms that do both. They combine CRM and DMS functionality, promising something spectacular. But these "all-in-one" systems can fall short, even though they have made tremendous progress over the last few years toward the dream of the perfect all-in-one system, and I'll give credit where credit is due, they are getting closer. They promise convenience, but some come with trade-offs in usability, innovation, and customization.

Alternatively, some brokers opt for separate CRM and DMS, utilizing what is known as "best-in-class" solutions for each. In other words, instead of looking for a solution with all the answers, they look at two different solutions, doing each task exceptionally. Given no all-in-one system and no two independent CRM and DMS systems are perfect, it begs the question: Why do some choose separate systems?

Firstly, because it means flexibility. Markets evolve, and so will your business. Having independent systems gives you the flexibility to switch one without blowing up the other. Outgrow your DMS? You can change it without losing your marketing engine. Want a better CRM? You're not tied to whatever's bundled with your brokerage. Secondly, it creates continuity. When you move brokerages or networks (and many do), your DMS often changes, but your CRM doesn't have to. A separate CRM protects your data and your pipeline. It gives you business continuity through transitions. Many brokers love the CRM component of an all-in-one solution and will use a separate DMS. In other cases they love the DMS component of an all-in-one solution and will use a separate CRM. No matter what combination you choose, you are in the driver's seat and need to choose what is best for your business.

That being said, separation does come with added responsibility. Integrations need to be set up and maintained. You may need third-party tools or even some light tech support. But for many brokers who are serious about growth, this modular setup creates a more agile, future-proof business. The bottom line is that your DMS is for funding deals and your CRM is for building relationships. Both matter, but they're built for different jobs. You should be aware of the difference and either intentionally build both systems, or commit to an all-in-one system; either way, the best system is the one that you are going to use. With that in mind, let's take a look at a few of the "best-in-class" features for CRM and DMS separately.

Features to Consider for CRM Systems

A CRM isn't just a fancy database; it's the heartbeat of your client experience and long-term business strategy. But not all CRMs are created equal. Some are bloated with features you'll never use, while others miss critical components that could save you time, protect you legally, and help you scale. So, to help you find the right CRM tech to use, here are the core features that matter most for brokers, and why that is the case.

Performance Dashboards and Analytics

Your CRM should be more than a place to store contact info. It should help you run your business like a CEO. Look for platforms that offer:

- Custom dashboards showing your pipeline at a glance

- Lead source tracking to identify what's working

- Conversion funnels to spotlight bottlenecks
- Year-over-year trend reports to support smart hiring or scaling decisions

If you can't use your CRM to make data-driven decisions, it's not a true business tool; it's a glorified Rolodex.

Permanent Note Tracking

This one's non-negotiable. Every conversation, every commitment, and every change to the file must be documented and time-stamped in a permanent record. Why does it matter?

- It protects you legally in the event of a client complaint or a regulator inquiry.
- It ensures continuity if a team member is off or transitions.
- It gives you context when that client comes back five years later.

If your CRM doesn't let you track deal-related notes indefinitely (or if they're editable after the fact), it's a liability.

Email Aggregation

Your CRM should act like a command centre, not a silo. That means centralizing communication, not just with clients, but also with:

- Lenders
- Lawyers
- Appraisers
- Realtors
- Internal team members

This kind of threaded visibility allows anyone on your team to jump into a file and immediately understand what's happening, without digging through inboxes.

Customization (But Be Careful)

CRMs like Zoho, HubSpot, and Salesforce offer deep customization. That can be a gift or a trap. It's tempting to build a system that tracks every possible client field, every possible milestone, every conceivable automation. But in practice, overbuilt CRMs can paralyze your team. If logging a note or moving a file takes five clicks, no one will do it consistently. Here's my pro tip: Stick to the 80/20 rule. Build for the 80% of files you handle regularly and give yourself breathing room for exceptions. Customization is powerful. Just use it wisely.

Brokerage/Network Portability

This is a quiet killer that most brokers don't think about until they need to make a move. If your CRM is tied directly to your brokerage or network, and you don't retain access or portability, you risk losing:

- Your pipeline

- Your task reminders

- Your database segmentation

- Your nurture campaigns

- Your entire client history

This is your business infrastructure. You need to own it. When evaluating CRM options, portability should be a core requirement, not a nice-to-have. At the end of the day, the best CRM for your business is the one that you and your team will actually use. It should streamline communication, safeguard your legal footing, give you visibility into your business, and grow with you, not weigh you down.

Features to Consider for DMS Systems

Your Deal Management System is where the rubber meets the road. It's the engine room of your mortgage practice. This is where deals get submitted, documents are tracked, lender conditions are managed, and client files are finalized. If your DMS isn't pulling its weight, you'll feel it in bottlenecks, compliance headaches, and frustrated clients. Here's what to look for when choosing or evaluating your DMS.

Portability

Just like with CRMs, this might be the single most overlooked issue when choosing a DMS: What happens if you switch brokerages? Some systems are proprietary to a specific network or tied directly to a brokerage license. That means:

- You lose access the moment you leave

- You risk disruption to in-progress files

- You lose valuable notes, documents, and lender responses

Look for a DMS that you can own or retain access to, either through your own license or as a standalone platform. Some DMS systems are portable, subject to your brokerage's approval, so make sure you get that approval when you join, so it's covered off up front. Portability protects your operations and your client experience during times of change. Don't make the mistake of not realizing how crucial it is.

Workflow Alignment

A great DMS doesn't just store deals, but enhances your team's workflow. It should:

- Mirror the stages you and your team follow from application to funding

- Allow for team collaboration with visibility into each file

- Offer role-based access so team members see what they need

- Help you triage files based on urgency, complexity, transaction type, or by lender

The best DMS platforms feel like an extension of your operations, not a clunky external step. If it contains too little or too much information, it won't improve workflow and will add a burden of additional administration.

Client-Facing Experience

A clean internal system is great, but don't forget what your client sees. Your DMS should offer:

- A simple, intuitive portal for clients to upload documents

- Clear task lists or status updates (ideally automated)

- Mobile accessibility for clients on the go

If your client finds your system frustrating or confusing, that reflects on your brand and not the software provider. A necessary practice is to have your team apply for a mortgage through a potential DMS. There is no better way to evaluate a DMS than experiencing it first-hand, like your clients will. Remember, first impressions matter. A smooth, branded experience goes a long way in building trust.

Document Collection

You shouldn't be hunting down documents one at a time by email. Instead, your DMS should:

- Let you request documents in structured lists

- Allow drag-and-drop uploading by clients

- Track what's been received vs. outstanding

- Automate follow-up reminders (ideally with customizable templates)

Anything that reduces the back-and-forth or manual chasing is a win for both your process and, most importantly, your client experience.

CRM Integration

Your DMS and CRM don't need to be married, but they definitely need to talk. This doesn't contradict what I said earlier: They still don't have to be on the same system, but they should be able to connect and draw from one another. Look for:

- Native integrations between your DMS and preferred CRM

- Zapier compatibility for automated handoffs

- Data mapping so that client info doesn't need to be re-entered

Redundant data entry is a productivity killer and a breeding ground for human error. Integration streamlines your processes and keeps everything in sync.

Digital Signing

If your DMS doesn't include a digital signing solution or integrate seamlessly with one like DocuSign, Adobe Sign, or OneSpan, that's a problem. You want:

- Embedded signing without needing to leave the platform

- Secure, trackable signature trails

- Templates for recurring docs (e.g., consent forms, disclosures)

In this day and age, digital signing isn't a luxury anymore. It's table stakes. Make sure it's baked into your DMS process.

The right DMS should feel like a productivity multiplier, not a daily annoyance. It should make your team more efficient, your clients better supported, and your entire pipeline more visible and manageable. The best part? When your DMS and CRM work together seamlessly, your entire business becomes more sellable, more repeatable, and more resilient.

CRM: An Investment, Not a Cost

One of the most common and costly mistakes brokers make is treating their CRM like a line item to minimize. Something to "get by" with. Something to choose based on monthly price, not long-term value. But here's the truth: Your CRM isn't just a tool. It's the digital backbone of your business, just like DMS. It's the system that holds every client interaction, every follow-up, every deal-related note, and every milestone in your customer lifecycle. It's what enables you to scale without sacrificing personalization, what protects your business in a compliance audit, and what keeps your pipeline warm months or even years after a deal closes.

That's not a cost. That's an investment.

Over the years, I've watched countless CRM systems rise and fall in Canada's mortgage space. Too often, brokers ride out those transitions and migrations with frustration, or worse, data loss. Every time a system collapses or becomes obsolete, businesses pay the price in dropped balls, broken workflows, and fractured client experiences. From my own journey as a broker, team leader, and eventually principal broker, I've learned the value of consistency. We changed brokerages. We changed DMS platforms. We even changed our brand name. But one thing stayed constant: our CRM.

That continuity was a lifeline. It meant our email sequences kept running. Our follow-up stayed intact. Our client records remained complete. There were no gaps in service, no apologies needed for missing birthdays or renewal dates. It gave us the foundation to grow confidently and the peace of mind that our client experience would remain intact, no matter what happened behind the scenes.

If you're serious about building a sellable, resilient mortgage business, don't just choose a CRM. Commit to it. Invest in it. Learn how to use it deeply. And make sure it's one you can grow with, not grow out of, because the brokers who win long-term aren't always the ones with the flashiest tech, they're the ones with the most consistent follow-up.

Political Realities: Mandated Tech and Admin

Let's not ignore the elephant in the room.

In the Canadian mortgage space, technology decisions aren't always made by brokers, and they're not always made based on what's the best fit for your business model. Some networks and brokerages mandate the use of certain platforms, backed by very compelling and, in many cases, reasonable rationales. Worse still, the rules often change and are not always transparent.

What's promised in the recruiting phase doesn't always reflect what's enforced on the ground, and what's enforced on the ground may vary dramatically, not just by brokerage, but by team.

Welcome to the wild west of mortgage tech.

This uneven landscape can put brokers in a tough position. You might find the "official" system doesn't align with your workflow, your CRM is better than the one provided, or the mandated DMS underdelivers, but using your preferred tool could trigger costs or compliance headaches. That's why doing your homework is critical. Don't just accept tech promises at face value. Ask specific questions and get answers in writing, such as:

- What tech is mandatory, and what's optional?

- Are there admin fees or penalties for using outside platforms?

- If I bring my own CRM, will I still get access to compliance support, training, and funding resources?

- How many brokers on the team use the mandated system, and how many don't? Why?

- What happens if my team doesn't like the new tech?

Better yet, talk to other brokers inside the organization. Seek out a mix of top producers, mid-level brokers, and newer brokers. Their experiences will tell you far more than a polished demo or recruiter pitch. In the end, your tech stack should serve your business, not the other way around, and while compromise is sometimes necessary, it should never come at the cost of long-term growth, operational sanity, or client experience.

Competition Drives Innovation

We're fortunate to work in a mortgage industry that's no longer dominated by a single platform. Back in 2008, Filogix held over 99% of the deal management market. Today, brokers have choices—and those choices are powerful. Tools like Boss, Filogix 2.0, Finmo, Hurricane and Velocity each bring unique strengths to the table. Some prioritize workflow and underwriting tools. Others focus on user experience or deep integrations. This diversity pushes the entire industry forward.

I'm proud to have contributed to that evolution. As a co-founder of a mortgage technology company, our goal from the start was to disrupt the DMS space and finally put the borrower first. That mission reshaped how tech companies in our space think about design, experience, and broker enablement. But disruption isn't a one-time act; it's an ongoing responsibility. Today, competition is what keeps every platform sharp and every provider accountable, and that's a win for brokers.

So, choose tools that reflect your way of working. Select platforms that support your vision, empower your team, and enhance your client experience because the right tech stack isn't just about moving files faster; it's about building long-term equity in your business.

Tech is not just support. It's a strategy. Make it count.

Free Download: Risk Preparedness Checklist

For a free downloadable checklist to evaluate your preparedness for business risks, go to: dougadlam.com/brokering

Or scan the QR code below:

Chapter 5

Branding—Because No One is Irreplaceable

In an industry built on trust and driven by word-of-mouth, your brand is more than a business card or website. Your brand is the sum total of every impression you leave behind. It's how you show up in conversations you're not part of. It's the reason clients choose you or forget about you. And yet, most brokers treat branding like a nice-to-have. They prioritize leads and conversions, systems, and volume. But here's the uncomfortable truth: Leads are temporary, systems evolve, and volume fluctuates.

Brands endure.

This chapter is about building something that lasts beyond your next funding month. Because even the best broker is ultimately replaceable, but a well-built brand is not. We'll dive into what branding really means (hint: it's not about ego), how to assess and refine your current brand, and how to create a brand that attracts the right clients, recruits the right people, and grows the right kind of equity.

We'll also break down brand architecture, explore the difference between a personal brand, a team brand, and an enterprise brand, and show you how to start no matter where you are in your journey. You can't out-hustle being forgettable, but you can build something unforgettable. Let's get to it.

What is Brand, Really?

In the mortgage broker business, most professionals start the same way: They market themselves by name. That's not necessarily a bad thing. In fact, it's a natural and practical entry point. Early in your career, when you're building your book of business, there's one thing you already have: a name that people know. It's natural and good to leverage existing relationships, spheres of influence, and professional networks. You introduce yourself as *"Jane Smith, Mortgage Broker,"* and the people in your life trust you, not your logo, not your tagline, not your brokerage. At this stage, your name is your brand, sort of.

Unfortunately, many brokers stay stuck there. They keep operating as if name recognition alone is enough to scale. They believe brand-building is something you do later, once you've "earned it," once the referrals are flowing, once the pipeline is full. But that's backwards and not the case at all. You don't build a brand *after* you become successful. You build a brand *to become* successful and to sustain that success in a way that's consistent, differentiated, and future-proof.

Let's be clear about something: Your name is not your brand. It might be a part of it, even a central part, but unless that name stands for something or is tied to a clear promise, a defined experience, and a recognizable identity, it's just a placeholder. And all placeholders are replaceable. The idea that "you are your brand" has been deeply ingrained in sales-driven industries like real estate, insurance, and finance, and while there's some truth in it, the danger is in mistaking visibility for equity. Just because people know your name doesn't mean they understand your value. Just because someone recognizes your photo on a billboard doesn't mean they can explain what makes your approach different or why they should refer you over the next person.

That's the gap branding fills.

A true brand is a strategy, not just a style. It's how your business shows up through service, through communication, and through consistency. It's the voice your emails carry. It's how your clients feel during the mortgage process. It's what leaders say behind closed doors when your name comes up. And it's very different from marketing. Marketing is how you get attention. Branding is why people trust your business once they're paying attention.

Think of a recent referral you received; someone you were told to call because "they're the best." What made you trust that recommendation? It wasn't because they had great business cards or a cool Canva template. It was because the person referring them attached their reputation to that name. They gave you more than contact info. They gave you a signal: "This person is good. You can trust them. They'll take care of you."

That is branding.

The moment someone refers you and attaches their own credibility to yours, that's brand equity at work. And the brokers who build equity intentionally are the ones who earn more referrals, attract stronger partners, and scale with stability. But here's where the industry often leads you astray: it glorifies hustle culture. It teaches you to chase the next deal, the next lead, the next week's pipeline. You get caught in survival mode, working in the business, not on the business. Branding becomes a "nice-to-have" for later, instead of a critical asset for right now.

This mindset is the great divide between a sales practice and a sellable business. A sales practice is fragile. It's tied to your personal energy, your daily output, and your name. The minute you step away, whether to take a vacation, to train your team, or to plan for the future, production drops. There's no leverage. No system. No legacy. A sellable business, on the other hand, is different. It's rooted in a brand that's bigger than any one person. It's built with intention, structured for growth, and designed to be understood by clients, partners, and team members alike, and that's where true enterprise value starts to form.

So, let's revisit the question: What is a brand, really? It's not a logo. It's not a color scheme. It's not a clever slogan or a slick Instagram feed. Those are tools. Assets. Wrapping paper. Your brand is your identity in the market. It's the perception you create, the promise you fulfill, and the reputation you carry. It's what makes someone say:

- She always calls back.

- He made things easy.

- They actually cared.

- I send all my clients to them.

If you're not intentionally shaping that identity, you're not truly in control of your business. You're letting the market define your brand for you based on random interactions, fragmented impressions, or assumptions. And when that happens, you're leaving value on the table, not just in the form of deals or commissions, but in the long-term equity that comes from building something bigger than yourself. So, remember, branding isn't an extra. It's not a vanity exercise. It's not a luxury for when you "have time." It's the foundation for everything that comes next.

Brokers Are Replaceable, Brands Are Not

This is the part nobody wants to hear, but every successful broker eventually learns: In the eyes of the market, most brokers are interchangeable. That might sound harsh, but it's the reality of our industry. Clients are flooded daily with advertisements from banks, rate aggregators, mortgage "specialists," and fintech platforms promising speed, ease, and rock-bottom rates. It's not personal. It's noise. And unless you've given your clients a reason to remember you, something beyond rate or speed, then your name becomes just another name in the crowd. That's the uncomfortable truth: Competence doesn't always win. Visibility doesn't always win. Value doesn't always win.

But brands do.

When your brand is weak, you're reduced to a commodity. You become a walking rate sheet, someone who gets one call among three, asked only, "What can you offer me?" There's no loyalty, no connection, and no stickiness. If another broker shows up with a slightly lower rate or a shinier ad, you're out. Not because you weren't good, but because you weren't remembered. On the flip side, when your brand is strong, you're not just remembered, you're championed!

Clients don't just recall your name, they recall how you made them feel. Partners don't just recommend you, they endorse you with confidence. Your name becomes shorthand for *trust, clarity, and results*, and that's when your brand starts working for you, even when you're not in the room. A strong brand gets referrals you didn't ask for, wins repeat business without chasing, attracts partners who align with your values, and justifies your process, your pricing, and your time.

Your brand becomes a defensive moat and an offensive tool, shielding you from commoditization while positioning you for growth. We've all seen it happen: a newer broker, still green, swoops in and wins a client that should have been yours. Not because they're better but because they were faster, more visible, undercut you, or simply louder in that moment. It hurts, but it also highlights the danger of being a name without an identity. This is why branding is not just about ego or aesthetics; it's about equity.

You can be incredibly skilled, but if no one can articulate what makes you unique, you're one comparison away from being forgotten. However, when your brand is intentionally built and rooted in values, consistent in its voice, and clear in its promise, it becomes magnetic. Clients stop shopping around. Referral partners stop hedging. They come to you because they know exactly what to expect, and they want your experience. The difference is loyalty. A client loyal to a name will leave for a lower rate, but a client loyal to a brand will stay, refer, and advocate, even when the competition tries to undercut you.

I'm not suggesting you erase your name from your business altogether. I'm simply suggesting you infuse your name with meaning. That's the difference between a salesperson who happens to do mortgages, and being a business that clients trust and remember. So, let's stop pretending everyone's irreplaceable, because they're not. But brands? Strong brands last, scale, and sell. So, let's build that kind of brand.

Don't Brand for Ego, Brand for Equity

Unfortunately, branding often gets mistaken for vanity. Too many brokers treat branding like a personal spotlight, a way to look successful, sound important, or project a curated image to the world. "Let's get some headshots. Let's make my Instagram look sleek. Let's put my face on a billboard." Now, I'm not saying that any of these things are inherently wrong. Aesthetics matter, and first impressions count. But if your brand is built primarily on you looking cool or your desire to feel important, you've missed the mark.

The true purpose of branding should always be equity, and not ego. Brand equity refers to the tangible and intangible value associated with being recognized, respected, and trusted in the market. It's what allows your business to attract clients organically, command higher-quality partnerships, and sustain long-term growth without burning you out. It's what gives your business structure, identity, and resilience, especially when you're not the one shaking hands, answering emails, or chasing leads.

If your brand is just your name slapped across every asset and your face is the centerpiece of every ad, then you're not building a business, you're building a personal sales practice. And while that can be profitable, it's not transferable, or sellable. It's built around you, and that means it falls apart without you. So, as you're creating a brand, ask yourself some important questions:

- Could someone else step into your brand and carry it forward? If the answer is no, then you're not building equity, you're building dependence.

- Could this business run and grow without your face on every file, flyer, and funnel? If not, your system may be too personality-driven and not process-driven.

- Would your client experience be consistent with or without you in the chair? If the answer is shaky, your brand may not be built for longevity.

Now, let's be clear: There's nothing wrong with being the face of your business, especially at the start. In fact, it's often a smart strategy. You are your greatest marketing asset when you're new. People trust people, and they especially trust people they know. So, leading with your name and story can create strong early traction. But the longer you stay in that mode, the more you trap yourself inside a brand that can't grow beyond your bandwidth. What if you bring on a partner or scale the team? What if you take a sabbatical? What if you want to sell your book of business five or ten years down the line? If you are the brand and your presence is required for the machine to run, you're not building an asset; you're building a treadmill.

Real brand equity means that your business becomes more than you. It has a message, a voice, a client promise, and a system that can be taught, scaled, and trusted, even when you're not in the room. Here's what that kind of brand unlocks:

- **Scalability:** A clear brand allows you to delegate without diluting quality. New team members can adopt your systems, tone, and client experience.

- **Transferability:** Whether you bring on new leadership or pass the torch, your business continues to operate with clarity and consistency.

- **Saleability:** A brand that doesn't rely on your name or face can be packaged and sold. That's real equity, and it's what separates a business from a personal hustle.

If you're serious about growing something that will outlive you and will generate value without you, step away from any ego-based branding. Start building a brand that reflects your promise and not your personality. That's how you move from being a broker to being a brand.

Brand Architecture

Once you've accepted that your brand is more than your name, more than your photo, slogan, or favorite font, the next question becomes: What kind of brand are you building? In the mortgage space, brand architecture generally falls into one of three categories: personal, team, and enterprise. Let's take a closer look at each and the pros and cons that accompany them.

Personal Brand

This is the most common starting point for brokers and originators. It's built around a single person, for example, *Jane Doe Mortgages* or *Mortgages by John*. The marketing, communication, and client relationship are all tied to the individual broker's identity. Pros? It creates fast trust-building with personal networks, it's easier to market authentically and consistently because you're speaking as yourself, and it's great for sole proprietors and solo operators.

On the other hand, the cons include that it's very difficult to scale, as clients prefer to work with you and not your team members, and it's more difficult to recruit other brokers to join your team down the road.

It's also harder to delegate without losing control or consistency, and it has low transferability, meaning that if you leave or retire, the brand will most likely die. A personal brand is ideal when you're just getting started, and your biggest asset is your own reputation, but if you plan to build something that outgrows you, like a team, a book of business, or a legacy, it has natural limitations.

Team Brand

A team brand shifts the focus from an individual to a collective. Think *Champion Mortgage Group* or *The Adam Financial Team*. Everyone works under one brand voice, one set of values, and ideally, one unified client experience, even if each originator brings their own personality to the table. Pros? It's easier to scale without diluting the client experience, and it encourages internal collaboration and shared accountability. It also means that clients learn to trust the process and the brand, and not just one person.

The cons? It requires very strong leadership and brave governance, it can cause inconsistencies between team members and erode brand equity, and it is more complex. Marketing, training, and even operations will require more input and intentionality to ensure that everyone is aligned with the brand voice and values.

A team brand works best when you're growing past solo capacity and want to build infrastructure that lasts, whether that's a team of salespeople, underwriters, assistants, or all three. But make no mistake: Building a team brand requires effort. You'll need documented standards, regular training, and a commitment to aligned messaging across every touchpoint.

Enterprise Brand

Enterprise brands are typically the umbrella brokerages or national firms that brokers join. These entities often provide national marketing support, technology platforms, compliance frameworks, and training programs. The pros? It comes with built-in credibility and consumer trust, it has national campaigns and support infrastructure, and compliance and legal resources are often more robust.

The cons? There will be less differentiation, and your brand might feel like one of many. In many cases, there will also be limited control over the branding itself, including colors, messaging, and tone. Lastly, consumer loyalty may sit with the brokerage and not with you. Enterprise branding can be powerful when combined with a strong personal or team identity, but brokers who rely solely on enterprise branding often find themselves invisible in a sea of sameness. The clients often remember the national name, not yours, unless you build your brand within the brand name

With all of this in mind, it begs the question: How do I choose? There's no one-size-fits-all approach to brand architecture. What matters most is aligning your structure with your long-term vision. If you want to stay solo and local and build a tight-knit referral business, keep it personal. If you're dreaming of a team that can run without you, a team brand is the way to go. If you're planning to plug into national infrastructure while keeping your own voice, find the right enterprise partner and define how your identity fits within theirs. Whatever you choose, do so with intention. Don't just default to what your brokerage offers or what everyone else is doing. Ask yourself:

- What kind of business do I want to build?

- How do I want clients to experience that brand?

- What happens to my brand if I take a month off, or five years off?

When your brand architecture supports your future goals and not just your current capacity, you set yourself up for growth, resilience, and the freedom to evolve.

What Are You Going to Compete On?

When choosing your brand, you are ultimately making a fundamental decision: What do you want to be known for? In our industry, the competitive triangle is familiar: Price, Speed, and Quality. The truth? It's important to make one of these your strength, and you can usually deliver on two, but very, very rarely is it possible to do all three at once. The strongest businesses choose consciously and build around that choice. Let's break it down.

Price a.k.a. Rate

In mortgage brokering, price almost always comes down to rate. Brokers know that some lenders offer a lower rate in exchange for a thinner commission. If your entire model revolves around being the lowest-rate provider, be honest about the trade-offs:

- You'll sacrifice revenue and long-term profitability.

- You'll struggle to attract and keep experienced, high-performing brokers.

- You'll risk turning your business into a commodity, and just another rate in a list.

That doesn't mean price doesn't matter. It does. Pricing strategy also includes decisions around broker fees, especially in private, alternative, and B-lending. There are plenty of opinions on when and how much brokers should charge. I'm not here to settle that debate. I'm simply here to relay this truth: The best brokers have the ability to charge more—ethically and within reason—while putting the client first. That ability reflects the value they provide, not just the cost of service.

Speed

Speed means responsiveness, efficiency, and urgency. Things like:

- How fast you return calls, texts, and emails

- How quickly you respond to new leads

- How fast you provide advice, get an approval in place, or close a deal

In today's market, speed is a serious competitive lever, especially with tighter closing windows and higher borrower stress. But speed without skill is dangerous. Quick answers don't mean correct answers. Fast file submission doesn't mean well-prepared files. The brokers who win on speed win because they balance it with competence and not just hustle for hustle's sake.

Quality a.k.a. Value

Quality is the hardest to define, but the most powerful to build your business around. It includes:

- Depth and clarity of advice

- Professionalism and expertise

- Reliability and repeatability of the process

- Accuracy, ethics, and client-first conduct

- Added value beyond the closing of the mortgage itself.

The challenge? Most borrowers can't spot quality right away. They may not know if the advice is good or bad until much later. That's why it takes intention to compete on quality. As a brand, you have to make it obvious, consistent, and part of every touchpoint.

So, with this in mind, it begs the question: Why do borrowers gravitate to price and speed? It's because a rate is easy to understand and speed is easy to notice. Value, on the other hand, requires explanation, context, and storytelling. Most borrowers don't show up saying, "I want to pay more for better advice." They default to what's visible and obvious: "What's the rate, and how fast can you get it done?" It's your job to create a brand that shows them why your guidance is worth more than just the cheapest option, unless, of course, that's the pond you decide to swim in.

Let's take an example from a different field. Imagine you need some dental work done, and you have two options: a qualified, experienced dentist who charges a normal rate or a medical student who offers a significantly cheaper rate. In this example, the benefit of paying more for a higher quality service is clear: less pain and fewer complications down the road. Sure, the medical student might be cheaper, but would you be willing to let someone unqualified work on your teeth just to save a few bucks?

The same goes for the mortgage process, but the downsides of a lower quality service are less obvious. However, they are very real and include things like stress, sleepless nights, confusion, chaos, and, in some cases, added costs down the line. Some people will be willing to accept these kinds of trade-offs, and others won't. Both kinds of clients exist. You get to decide which ones you want to attract.

Every business feels the temptation to chase all three. They want to be the fastest, cheapest, and best, but that's a trap. Trying to win on price, speed, and quality at the same time usually leads to mediocrity in all three. Instead, pick a lane and build around it. Here's what that might look like in practice:

- **If you compete on price**, you'll need a lean, efficient operation. High volume. Heavy automation. You'll also have to accept client churn and thinner margins.

- **If you compete on speed**, you'll need fast systems, sharp tech, and a focus on lower-complexity files where responsiveness matters most.

- **If you compete on quality**, you'll need to invest more time with each client. Build trust and educate them, and in exchange, you'll earn stronger margins and long-term loyalty.

All of these are valid business models, but you should only focus on one initially. Choose deliberately. Even though value and expertise aren't always visible on a spreadsheet, they can make a visible impact on your business. How? By using case studies, reviews, and testimonials that highlight real client wins, and by embracing consistency and performance. If your value isn't obvious at first glance, make sure it becomes obvious through every client touchpoint.

Once you've taken the time to turn one of these models into your main strength, you can start to think about bringing in a second one to complement it and develop your competitive edge. ,

Brand Touchpoints

When most brokers think about branding, they imagine logos, websites, and maybe a social media profile picture. But the truth is, your brand isn't just what you design; it's what you deliver. And it shows up everywhere. Your brand lives in the tiny details just as much as in the big, visible ones. In fact, it's often the smallest touchpoints, the ones people barely notice consciously, that leave the most lasting impressions. Here are just a few of the places your brand appears:

- **Your website:** Is it clear, professional, and easy to navigate? Does it reflect your personality and values? Or does it feel like a generic template with no soul?

- **Your email signature:** Is it clean, informative, and aligned with your visual identity? Or is it cluttered, outdated, or inconsistent?

- **Your voicemail greeting:** Is it friendly, confident, and professional? Or does it sound rushed, robotic, or worse—non-existent?

- **Your intake process:** How smooth is the experience when a new client starts working with you? Are they impressed by how organized and thoughtful it is, or left wondering what happens next?

- **Your client follow-up:** Do you follow through reliably and on time? Do your communications sound like you or like a stock template copied and pasted without thought?

- **Your communication style:** Whether it's you or your team, how you write, speak, and respond sends a message. Are you warm, competent, responsive, and consistent? Or are you scattered, reactive, and impersonal?

- **Your WOW moments:** The moments where your team goes above and beyond client expectations. It's a combination of planned wow moments and those where your team is empowered to do unbelievable things, causing lasting impact.

Each of these moments is a brand touchpoint—a chance to show your client who you are and what they can expect from you—and together, these touchpoints shape your reputation far more than any single marketing campaign ever could. Most brokers waste these opportunities. They treat them as functional rather than intentional. They respond to emails without tone. They slap together onboarding forms that feel cold or confusing. They let voicemail greetings go months without being updated.

But the top producers? The brokers who build brands that last? They pay attention. They know that every client interaction, no matter how small, is a chance to reinforce their brand promise. Because branding isn't about being flashy. It's about being consistent, intentional, and memorable at every level. So ask yourself:

- What experience do people have at every stage of working with me?

- Do my systems and tools reflect my values and professionalism?

- Are my touchpoints helping people trust me, or leaving them with question marks?

You don't need to overhaul everything at once. Just start noticing and refining, one touchpoint at a time. Because when you treat every interaction as an extension of your brand, you stop being just another mortgage broker and start being someone unforgettable.

Start Where You Are

You don't need a rebrand to start building a stronger brand. You don't need a new logo, a fresh website, or the perfect tagline. What you need is clarity. Clarity about:

- **Who you are:** Your values, your voice, your differentiators.

- **Who you serve:** The audience you're built for, and what matters most to them.

- **What promise you make:** What people can expect from working with you, every time.

- **How you deliver on it:** Not just once, but consistently, across every touchpoint.

You can start right now with your next client call, your next follow-up email, your next referral thank-you. That's where brand is built: not in theory, but in action.

Free Download: Competitive Positioning Worksheet

For a free downloadable worksheet to map where you compete today—on rate, speed, or value—and where you want to be, go to: dougadlam.com/brokering

Or scan the QR code below:

Chapter 6

The Economics of Brand Equity

Once you've built a brand that stands for something, the real magic can begin. A strong brand does more than generate awareness or earn compliments; it creates leverage. Leverage in your pricing. Leverage in your hiring. Leverage in your negotiations. And, over time, leverage in the value of your business itself. Most brokers don't realize how deeply brand equity impacts their bottom line. They see branding as a marketing function, not a financial asset. But the truth is, your brand is one of the few things in this business that grows in value as you grow. It doesn't just grow in volume, but in credibility, reputation, and influence.

In this chapter, we'll explore the financial upside of building a recognizable, trusted, and differentiated brand. Not just to attract more business, but to increase the worth of the business behind it. We'll unpack the link between brand and pricing power, brand and recruiting, and how the brand foundations can directly influence your business's operational efficiency, retention, and long-term exit value. Because in this industry, deals come and go. But brand equity, when real and long-lasting, can pay dividends every day.

Pricing Power

Before we can truly grasp the financial value of brand equity, we need to remember what the previous chapter was all about: Your brand is not you. Even if you're a solo broker or someone without a support team, the brand you're building is bigger than just your name. If you want to build, scale, and sell, it has to be more than just your name and a reflection of your personality. It needs to be an entity with its own voice, values, reputation, and presence in the marketplace. Yes, that identity may begin with you. But if you want your business to grow beyond that, then you need to begin thinking of your brand as a living asset and not a personal label.

You are not your business, and your business is not you. What you're building over time isn't just a database or a deal count, but brand equity. It's the cumulative value of how the market sees, trusts, and chooses you over the alternatives. That mindset shift is the dividing line between a producer and a business builder. Without it, you're stuck in a cycle of chasing deals, relying on your personal hustle, and competing almost entirely on price.

The reality is that in the absence of a brand, you will always compete on rate. That's the default position of an undifferentiated mortgage broker. No matter how talented or experienced you are, if your business has no distinct identity, no emotional, strategic, or experiential edge, then your prospects will compare you on the one variable they do understand: the interest rate. And in that race to the bottom, there are no winners. But a strong brand can change the equation.

When your brand is trusted—when it carries the weight of reputation, professionalism, expertise, and consistency—then the rate becomes secondary. Clients aren't just choosing a mortgage; they're choosing a process, a promise, and a feeling. They're choosing you, but more importantly, they're choosing what the brand represents. Think of luxury cars. Think of your favorite boutique coffee shop. Think of the advisors, professionals, and service providers you trust implicitly. Are they the cheapest option? Likely not, but they are valued. Why? Because their brand evokes quality, care, and confidence, and that perceived value gives them pricing power.

The same is true for mortgage brokers. A strong brand allows you to charge appropriately for the value you deliver, stand firm when others are discounting just to close, attract clients who are looking for service and not just savings, and most importantly, increase your profit margin while doing work you're proud of. When you stop viewing your brand as a decoration and start treating it as a strategic business asset, you unlock a different kind of growth. This growth is one that isn't tethered to the lowest rate but rooted in long-term value. That's the power of brand equity.

Recruiting and Retention

Strong brands don't just attract clients, but they also attract great people. Whether you're looking to build a small support team, grow a group of brokers under your leadership, scale a full brokerage, or even lead a national network, the principle is the same: People want to align with brands they believe in. That belief is what drives commitment. It's what turns employees, agents, and partners into ambassadors. It's what makes your culture feel magnetic. Not because of the pay structure or the tech stack, but because of what your brand stands for.

This is the often-overlooked power of brand equity: It fosters a sense of belonging, clarity, and pride. When people feel proud to represent a brand, they stay longer, perform better, and recruit others to join the team. That's not just culture; that's operational efficiency and long-term value. Now flip that around. If your business is just a collection of individuals doing deals under a shared logo, that's not a brand; it's a transaction engine. And the moment someone leaves, they take their energy, clients, and value with them. No shared mission. No loyalty. No long-term retention. It's a revolving door of talent, and over time, that churn becomes expensive, both financially and in terms of reputation.

This dynamic shows up even inside large brokerage brands. I've seen it firsthand. Within the same national brokerage, it's not uncommon for brokers to move between teams, even while keeping the same provincial license and brokerage name. At first glance, that might seem odd. Why switch teams if the umbrella brand is the same? Because the experience isn't the same. Teams within brokerages often operate with very different values, standards, processes, and cultures, even if their signage and business cards look identical. The brand equity of each team is distinct. One might focus on education and long-term planning; another might lead with speed and volume. One might prioritize collaboration; another might be built around individual performance.

When brokers shift teams, it's often not about personal conflict, but rather about brand alignment. They're trying to find a brand experience that resonates, a culture they can see themselves thriving in, and a leader whose vision they believe in. During my time in a national Strategic Growth role, I had countless conversations with brokers who were navigating these very decisions. I've also experienced it on the front lines, leading teams, welcoming talent, and watching some choose to move on. It's part of the evolution. Brokers are constantly seeking their tribe, their values, and their purpose.

But here's what I've learned: Those who stop chasing someone else's brand and start building their own brand equity are the ones who grow faster, last longer, and build something meaningful. Because great brands don't just retain talent; they grow it. They create environments where people are proud to belong, where they see a future, and where the brand becomes their brand, too. That kind of buy-in isn't just good for culture. It's good for business.

Operational Leverage

One of the most underrated superpowers of a strong brand is its ability to positively impact internal operations. That's right. Branding isn't just an external way to attract clients or build credibility in the market. It's something that affects the way your business is run. When you've taken the time to articulate your brand's DNA, including the mission, values, tone, ideal client profile, and unique approach, so many other decisions that used to seem hard will fall into place and become automatic. Simple questions like, "Who do we serve and who don't we?" can add tremendous value and provide clarity on how your business operates. Other questions that can help include asking yourself what you value as a brand and what you're willing to walk away from. How do you do things? How do you speak to clients and follow up? How do you deal with tight deadlines and stress? Simple questions like these mean that the answers are no longer up for debate. They are answered and part of the daily operations, which provides leverage.

Brand clarity creates decision clarity, and decision clarity creates operational efficiency. Instead of reinventing the wheel every time you onboard a new team member, launch a campaign, or respond to an unusual client request, you have a compass. A framework. A filter. That's how great brands scale without sacrificing quality. They remove ambiguity from the inside out. With a strong brand foundation in place, you will reduce:

- **Decision fatigue:** Your team isn't constantly guessing what "right" looks like

- **Onboarding time:** New hires get up to speed faster and align with your vision more easily

- **Managerial friction:** Because systems and standards are built into the brand

- **Client inconsistency:** Your brand promise shows up in every interaction, no matter who's delivering it

That kind of consistency is what makes a business feel stable to both clients and partners. The bottom line is that without a strong brand, you'll have to rely on hustle to keep things afloat. That might work at first, but hustle burns out while brands can scale, compound, and provide leverage. That leverage is what allows you to accomplish more with less effort, less friction, and less oversight. It's the difference between being busy and being in control.

Brand Equity Drives Exit Value

Let's talk about the endgame for a second. What happens when you want out? Whether you plan to sell your business, step back from day-to-day operations, or simply reduce personal involvement over time, the brand you've built (or didn't build) will determine how easy the transition will be. Brand equity is the most important thing you can build because if it can outlive the founder, so can the rest of the business. If you build a brand on its own equity, market, and systems, it's something that can be packaged, passed on, or even sold.

When people trust the brand, not just the broker, continuity becomes possible, providing you with the out you're looking for. Brand equity also creates leverage in negotiations. Whether you're selling, merging, or onboarding a successor, your brand's reputation becomes a major point of value. Brand equity gives you options, and without it, your only real path to retirement is slowly winding down or handing your database to someone else. Often for far less than you imagined.

The kicker is, very few mortgage professionals build sellable brands. Most build high-income sales practices with zero exit plan. That's not a judgment but an observation and a warning. If you're in this for a few quick years, that might not matter. But if you're building something that you want to last, something that you can scale and sell, your brand becomes your moat and your multiplier. When your name fades from the website and you're no longer present in every client meeting, your brand will remain. The sooner you start building that brand with intention and strategy, the more value it will hold when you need it most.

What Brand Equity Looks Like

Brand equity can seem like a vague or lofty concept, especially in an industry where performance is often measured deal by deal. But in practice, brand equity is unmistakable. It shows up in the way your business operates, the way people talk about you, and the resilience your company shows when you're not in the room. You know a broker has strong brand equity when:

- **Clients refer them without hesitation:** Not because of a great rate, but because of a great experience.

- **Competitors respect them (and talk about them):** Even if they're vying for the same clients or agents, there's a sense of admiration and recognition.

- **Recruiters and lenders know their name:** Not just because they do volume, but because they've built a consistent reputation for professionalism, integrity, and results.

- **They charge fairly and never apologize for it:** Because they've earned the trust and credibility that transcends the price conversation.

- **They could step away for a month, and the business still runs:** Not just limps along, but actually maintains momentum because systems, standards, and a brand promise are already in place.

That's the goal! Not just to be booked, busy, and breaking records, but to be valuable in a way that's durable, defensible, and transferable. If you want a quick gut-check on your current brand strength, ask yourself two hard but telling questions:

1. If I were to transition out of the business today, would the business suffer?

2. If we changed the name under which our business operates, would our clients or partners hesitate to work with us?

If the answer to both questions is *no*, congratulations. You've likely built a brand with real equity. That's rare in this business, and worth protecting. If the answer to either question is *yes*, don't panic. Brand equity isn't fixed. It's not something you either have or don't. It's something you build, day by day, decision by decision, touchpoint by touchpoint. That might mean developing clearer messaging. It might mean tightening your client experience. It might mean pulling your face off the website and promoting a team promise instead of a personal one.

Whatever the path, the work is worth it, because brand equity doesn't just elevate your business. It liberates you from it. When you've built something bigger than yourself, you've created more than a job. You've created an asset. One that works for you, whether you're in the office, on vacation, or planning your next chapter.

From Brand Equity to Business Equity

At a certain point, your brand stops being something that supports your business and starts being something that *is* your business. That's when brand equity transforms into business equity. Business equity is the real, tangible value of your company as an asset. It's what makes your business worth something beyond your own time, talent, and presence. It's what allows you to scale, to hire, to take time off, and eventually, to sell or pass the business on with confidence. Here's the key: Strong business equity is built on strong brand equity. When your brand is clear, consistent, and well-regarded in the market, it naturally feeds into the five pillars of business equity:

- **Pricing Power:** You're no longer competing on the lowest rate. You're competing on value. That directly improves margins.

- **Recruiting and Retention:** People want to work with you and for you because they believe in what you stand for.

- **Operational Leverage:** You don't have to make every decision or hold every relationship. Systems carry the weight.

- **Market Position:** You occupy a place in the client's mind that others can't easily take. That creates staying power and trust.

- **Scalability:** You can grow without diluting quality because the brand promise isn't tied to a single person, but is embedded in the business.

When these elements align, your business becomes more than a sales engine. It becomes a platform, one that has infrastructure, identity, and intrinsic value, even when you're not actively running the show. That's the difference between being self-employed and being a business owner. In the broker world, it's easy to mistake volume for value, but if the business only works when you work, then the asset isn't the business, it's you. That's fine for a time, but it's not sustainable and certainly not sellable.

If your long-term goal is to create something that lasts, something that could be sold, or at least successfully transitioned to someone else, then branding isn't a vanity project but an essential infrastructure. Your brand is what people remember and what your clients trust. It's what your team rallies behind and what your competitors recognize. When the brand becomes recognizable, referable, and reliable, it also becomes equity. It's not just brand equity, but business equity.

One thing to remember is that brand equity isn't just created in one bold move but rather built in moments of consistency. Every email you send, every referral call you take, every social post, client update, follow-up message, and lender conversation—it all adds up. Every time you reinforce your brand through action, communication, or experience, you're adding a brick to the foundation of long-term value. Like all forms of equity, brand equity compounds over time. The more intentional you are, the more momentum you will create. The more clarity you have, the more sellable your business becomes. Every small investment in your brand today becomes a multiplier for your business tomorrow.

Free Download: Value-Add Ideas Cheat Sheet

For a free downloadable cheat sheet with practical ideas to add value beyond rate, strengthen your brand, and increase equity in your business, go to: dougadlam.com/brokering

Or scan the QR code below:

PART TWO
SCALE

Chapter 7

Exit Planning From Day One

Most mortgage brokers enter the business with one goal in mind: close deals, earn income, and help people secure financing. There's nothing wrong with that goal. In fact, that's a worthy goal…at first. But if you're reading this book, it likely means you're aiming higher. You're starting to understand that brokering can be more than just a job. It can also be a business. One with systems, value, reputation, and, most importantly, potential for something beyond your own capacity. The truth is, very few brokers start with the end in mind. But the ones who do? They're the ones who build something that lasts.

Whether your dream is to sell your book, exit at a profit, transition your business to a partner or family member, or simply reduce your personal involvement over time, that vision won't just appear. It must be designed from the very beginning. You won't get a valuable business by accident. You get there by building something that can survive and thrive without you at the center of it. This chapter is all about making that shift. From earning commission to building equity. From chasing closings to creating a legacy.

We'll cover why early exit planning is essential, how to build a business (not just a book of clients), why delegation isn't optional, how valuation starts with vision, and how to reverse-engineer your success by designing with the end in mind. Remember, you're not just a broker. You're a builder. And if you build this right, your business can go far.

The Importance of Early Exit Planning

Exit planning is more than just preparing for a sale. It's about how you build your business, starting right here and now. It's the difference between creating a high-paying hustle and building a high-value company. Many brokers don't think about exit planning until they're burned out or thinking of retirement. But by then, it's often too late. They look around and realize they've built an incredibly successful business that depends entirely on them. It's their name, network, and energy keeping the place alive, and without them, there's not much left to sell.

The hard truth is that the mortgage business that dies when you step away was never really a business. It was just a job you owned. That's okay. No judgment here. If that's the goal, you're doing great! But if you're dreaming of something bigger and want to scale and sell one day, you need to plan for the exit long before you're ready to make the move. One of the paradoxes in our industry is that the income ceiling is so high that many brokers stay stuck chasing deals instead of designing growth. The commission cheques are good, sometimes even great, and that short-term success can mask the absence of a long-term strategy. But earning a strong income doesn't mean you're building a strong business.

One of the most frustrating aspects of this industry is that most brokers already do 80% of the work required to build a business. They invest in marketing, client relationships, software, and support teams. But they stop short of the last 20%. What does that last 20% entail? The strategic planning, documentation, and infrastructure that make the business sellable. The last 20% is where real equity lives.

Early exit planning forces your systems to be clean, documented, and transferable. It encourages you to do everything in a way that allows another person to step in and operate effectively. Early exit planning also ensures that your brand is bigger than your personal name and reputation, making it easier to scale without causing brand confusion. When you plan your exit early and effectively, it detaches your business income from your personal input. In other words, revenue can continue even when you're not always there or part of every client conversation. Additionally, early planning positions your business as an asset, rather than just a list of past clients.

Putting all of this together leads to one general truth: Exit planning is a form of business building. It doesn't mean you're stepping into something with one foot already out of the door. Instead, it means you're building something strategically, giving it your all so the business can run without you if that's what you choose to do. The good news is, if you've read this far, you're already ahead of the majority of the pack. Why? Because you're not just chasing deals, but are open to creating something that will outlast you. So, start today, but design it with the end in mind.

Build a Business, Not Just a Book

Building on what we've already discussed in previous chapters, we know that there's a big difference between building a book of business and building an actual business. A book is personal. It's a list of clients who trust you and who call you for advice. It's those people who rely on you for guidance and refer you to friends and family. Now, let's get something straight: I'm not saying that a book of business isn't valuable. It is absolutely vital! But it can also be limiting. As we've seen and discussed before, if the business is built entirely on you, it can't survive without you. And if it can't survive without you, it means that it's not transferable, and ultimately, not sellable.

A business, on the other hand, is a machine. It's a system that delivers value, earns trust, and grows, with or without you in every seat. If your goal is to build something that is sellable, which I believe it is, considering you're here reading this book, then your efforts can't stop at building a strong book. They need to continue into building a strong infrastructure process and identity beyond yourself. We've already touched on some things to keep in mind to help you create a business and not just a book, but to recap, here are three questions you can ask yourself to help align your actions with your goals:

1. If I took a month off, would the business survive or stall?

2. Could someone else be trained to do what I do, using the tools I've built?

3. Am I documenting what works or keeping it all in my head?

These questions are more than just thought exercises. They are also pressure tests for scalability. Too many brokers get stuck in the trap of "If I want it done right, I have to do it myself." That mindset may feel efficient in the short term, but it becomes a liability in the long term. If you're the only one who can run the ship, you've built a dependency, not a business. So, start thinking beyond the book that serves as a foundation, and begin to focus on the finish line. Sure, a great book might earn you a strong income, but a great business will earn you long-term value and can create multiple other opportunities. By building a business instead of a book, you're ultimately building your own freedom, allowing you the opportunity to step back, scale, or sell without skipping a beat.

Delegation Can Save Your Business

In the first chapter, I briefly mentioned my story and how I found my "why." But I would like to expand on the story a little bit more. Not because it's a story about growth, but because it's one of survival.

As I mentioned, in 2016, our team had the best year ever up to that point. More deals, higher margins, raving clients. On the surface, everything looked perfect. But behind the scenes, I was completely burned out. Not tired. Done. I hit the wall so hard I started planning an exit, not years down the road, but immediately. I brought the issue to my mastermind group, thinking they'd support my decision to walk away. Instead, they gave me a challenge that changed everything: "Delegate everything. Step back, hand over the reins, and see what happens."

So I did. I stepped back, reluctantly at first, waiting for disaster. Three days later, the business was still standing. Three weeks later? Thriving. Three months later? I realized that I had been the bottleneck. I thought that without me, the business would suffer, but in reality, I was holding them back. That experience taught me one of the most important lessons of my career, which was that scalability isn't just about systems, but also about your mindset.

The truth is, I should never have gotten to that point. I had started my business with the right intentions: I added team members, shared responsibilities, and built infrastructure. But somewhere along the way, I started holding on too tightly. I convinced myself that certain pieces could only be done by me, and that thinking nearly cost me the entire business. If you've been in the industry for any length of time, especially during the COVID years, you know what burnout feels like. And if you've ever reached the point where your inner monologue sounds like, "I'm not thinking of quitting. I am quitting," then you know how dangerous that moment can be. But it doesn't have to be that way.

Delegation isn't just a productivity hack, but a survival strategy. It's what turns a fragile business into a resilient one. It's how you create space to lead instead of grind. And it's one of the clearest indicators that your business can eventually exist without you at the center of it all. So, here's your takeaway: Don't wait for burnout to force your hand. Plan for delegation early. Build it into your growth strategy from day one. When you delegate with intention, you're not just protecting your time; you're protecting the future value of your business.

Why don't you take a moment right now and consider how you can delegate something within your business or life? It might be scary at first, but the more you let go of control and learn to trust, the more others will have the opportunity to step up and prove what they can do.

Valuation Starts With Vision

Most brokers don't start their careers thinking about business valuation. In fact, most don't think of themselves as business owners at all. Ask around and you'll hear it often:

"I am my business. My clients work with me and only me. I'll broker until the day I die, and my business will die with me." It's a common belief, but a limiting one, because if that's true, then what you've built isn't a business but a high-paying job with no succession plan. If you ever want to sell, step back, or pass it on, you'll be faced with a hard truth: You can't sell what only exists in your head.

If someone were to offer to buy your business tomorrow, what exactly would they be buying? A predictable revenue engine? A trained and empowered team? A repeatable client experience? Documented systems and workflows? A brand with market recognition and trust? Or are they just buying a book of clients that disappears the moment you do?

Early-stage brokers rarely ask these questions, and that's understandable. You're in build mode, focused on deals, relationships, and momentum. But the great brokers? The ones who scale, step back, and eventually exit? They ask those questions early, and they build with the answers in mind.

Valuation starts long before a business is listed for sale. It starts with vision. Your vision shapes how you spend your time, who you hire, what you delegate, and what you build. It dictates whether you invest in personal branding or business branding. It determines whether you hoard knowledge or systematize success. It also shapes whether you're building something that will last or something that will end with you. Future buyers might look for many things, but they don't really care about the personality. They want predictability. They're not seeking a superhero who can juggle every deal and client with unmatched skill. They're looking for a well-oiled machine—a business that runs on process, not personal charm. So start thinking like a business owner, not just a mortgage broker. Vision isn't just about where you want to go. It's about what kind of business you want someone else to want.

Design With the End in Mind

If you've read all of this and you're feeling overwhelmed because you haven't started thinking about the end, take a breather. You don't need to have every detail of your exit strategy mapped out from day one. You don't need to know when you'll exit, how you'll exit, or even to whom you'll sell or transition your business, but you do need to build like someone else will be taking over one day, because eventually they will. Whether it's a buyer, a business partner, your team, or even a family member, the ability to exit successfully hinges on how you design the business today.

If you're not sure where to start, start with a few critical questions and be honest with the answers:

- Are my systems simple, documented, and usable by others?

- Am I building a team that can function without me, or am I constantly involved and micromanaging their steps?

- Do I consistently track and understand the metrics that drive my business, or am I only focused on revenue?

- Are my financials clean, accurate, and accessible, or am I buried in spreadsheets only I can decipher?

- Is the brand I'm building strong enough to stand on its own, or will it fade when I remove myself from the equation?

These elements aren't just about preparing for an exit in the distant future; they're the exact same tools that make your life easier right now.

When you design a business with the end in mind, you also create a business that's more sellable, less stressful, and better equipped to grow. Here's a powerful exercise to keep yourself accountable:

If you had the money and opportunity to buy a mortgage business tomorrow, what would it need to have for you to say yes?

Think about it. Really think about it. What do you want to buy from others? Would you want a reliable, well-organized financial system? Would you want documented and repeatable client experiences? Would you want to buy a CRM that makes sense without needing further explanations? Would you want team members who are empowered to be independent? Perhaps you'd want to buy a system that is automated and reduces human error, or a referral pipeline that trusts the brand and not just a face? Whatever it is you would like to buy, build it.

Use this lens to build the kind of business that you would like to buy, because one day, someone else will evaluate it through that exact lens, and when they do, you want them to see more than just potential. You want them to see performance, structure, and real value. Designing with the end in mind isn't just about one day stepping away. It's about building something worth stepping away from.

Free Download: Delegation Scorecard Survey

For a free downloadable scorecard that reveals where you fall on the spectrum between salesperson and business owner, go to: dougadlam.com/brokering

Or scan the QR code below:

Chapter 8

Leadership Transitions— From Player to Coach

In the early days of building a mortgage business, your edge comes from personal hustle. You're the rainmaker—generating leads, closing deals, answering calls at all hours. You're the player on the field, taking every shot and making things happen. And for a while, that works. But eventually, hustle has a ceiling. If you want to grow, you have to step off the field. You have to shift from being the top performer to becoming the leader who builds other performers. That's right, you need to shift from player to coach.

This is one of the hardest transitions in the mortgage industry. Not because brokers lack drive, but because the very traits that made them successful (control, speed, personal ownership) are the same ones they have to unlearn. Leadership demands a different mindset, a different pace, and a willingness to let go in order to grow. In this chapter, we'll explore why so many brokers resist this shift, how to evolve from top seller to system builder, and what it really means to lead others. We'll talk about how to choose leadership, not as a title, but as a practice, and how to learn from those who've made the leap before you.

If you're feeling the limits of doing it all yourself, this chapter is your next play. Let's get you off the field and into the role of coach.

Why Brokers Resist the Shift

The transition from player to coach is one of the most pivotal and resisted moves in a broker's journey. It's not because brokers don't want to grow. It's because growth at this stage doesn't come from working harder; it comes from working differently, and that's uncomfortable. To overcome the resistance to this shift, we must first understand the reasons behind it. While it may vary from broker to broker, many struggle to step out of the player role for the same key reasons. Let's take a closer look at a few of these reasons:

- **Fear of losing control:** When you're used to touching every file, talking to every client, and making every decision, the idea of someone else stepping in can feel risky. What if they drop the ball? What if they don't represent the brand the way you would?

- **Belief that no one can match your client experience:** Brokers often take pride in the level of service they provide. That's a good thing, but it becomes a liability when it turns into, "I'm the only one who can do it right." That mindset keeps you trapped in every transaction.

- **Tying identity to performance:** For years, your value came from being the expert, the closer, the one who made it all happen. Stepping back can feel like losing your edge or abandoning what made you successful. But leadership isn't about being the best at everything; it's about building a team that can be.

- **Confusing activity with productivity:** In this industry, it's easy to equate being busy with being valuable. But activity for the sake of activity isn't the goal. Real value comes from creating systems, growing people, and building something that lasts beyond your daily output.

The truth is that staying stuck in player mode eventually limits your impact. You can't be the best player and the best coach at the same time, because you won't have the vantage point required to make the best calls for the whole team. When you refuse to let go, you become the bottleneck you've been trying to prevent. You become the reason things slow down and burn out, and you might even stifle growth. Leadership is a different game, and stepping into that role doesn't diminish your value; it multiplies it. When you let go of being the only player on the field, you unlock the ability to build a team, a business, and a legacy.

From Star Player to Systems Builder

It's fun being the star player on a team. You're the one building momentum, winning clients, and being at the top of your game. Your name is chanted by the crowds, and you're comfortable being the best. The truth is, a star player might win games, but it requires a coach to build dynasties. A coach doesn't run every play. They design the playbook, recruit talent, train consistently, and build a culture where people know their roles and play them well, but they don't score. They build the system to ensure that someone else does.

That's your new job as a leader, and giving up the spotlight and chanting crowd can be difficult. But that's what it takes if you're serious about building a business that delivers consistent value, with or without you. If you're planning on making the shift and aiming to scale your brokerage, there are a few things to keep in mind:

Firstly, you need to document repeatable processes. The magic can't just live in your head. If you have a winning recipe, this is where you decide to write it down and turn it into a practical tool others can use as well. You're no longer focusing on making sure that you're the best; you're focusing on making sure that everyone around you is doing their best. If something is working, capture it. Write it down. Build it into your workflow. Whether it's how you qualify leads, manage files, or communicate with referral partners, make it system-dependent and not person-dependent.

Secondly, you need to identify and train your future leaders. Who is taking over as captain? Who might be taking over as the next star or even assistant coach? No great business runs on one leader forever. Look for those on your team who are already showing initiative, who care about clients and culture, and start developing them now. Leadership is a muscle, and it gets stronger with trust and training.

The third thing you should do is to let go of control and perfectionism. This one is a hard one, I know. When your name is on the business or when you have high stakes invested, it's natural to want to control everything and have it done your way. But leadership means trading ego for impact. Good systems allow for consistency, even if things aren't done exactly the way you would have done them. Remember, in very few cases is there only one right way to approach something. Just because it's different doesn't mean it's automatically wrong.

Lastly, you need to build systems that enable delegation. If you can't delegate, you can't scale. That doesn't mean dumping tasks and walking away without a care in the world. It means designing systems that guide action and empower people. It means trusting your team and ensuring they have the necessary tools to succeed. This means no micromanaging, but rather putting faith in your system and trusting your team.

Making this shift isn't about lowering the bar. Quite the opposite, actually. It's about raising it. You're not abandoning quality; you're scaling it. When your business runs on systems instead of your stamina, you create a foundation that can grow, adapt, and thrive long after you've stepped off the field.

Coaching Is Its Own Discipline

Making the leap from player to coach isn't just a shift in job title; it's a transformation in how you think, act, and lead. Being a top producer doesn't automatically make someone a great coach. In fact, some of the best players struggle the most with this shift. Why? Because coaching is a completely different discipline. It's no longer about being the expert, but about drawing out the expertise in others. To become an effective coach, you need to develop an entirely new skill set. These aren't soft skills; they are scale skills. They are the skills that allow your business to grow beyond your own capacity and capability. Here are a few skills you'll need as a newly appointed coach:

- **Communication Skills:** Coaching starts with clarity. You must set clear expectations, provide timely feedback, and paint a compelling vision that your team can rally behind. Great coaches don't leave people guessing. Instead, they provide a clear framework for action and accountability.

- **Emotional Intelligence:** Leading people means understanding people. You'll need to recognize emotions, navigate conflict with empathy, and support growth in ways that are personalized and meaningful. Some days you're a strategist, other days a mentor, and often both in the same conversation.

- **Strategic Thinking:** As a coach, you're not focused on the next file; you're focused on the next quarter, the next hire, the next evolution of your team. You need to see around corners, plan for capacity, and stay agile as the market shifts. Strategy becomes your new daily work. You need to consciously step away from getting stuck into deals and let your team dig deep and figure it out. Even if it means a mistake or failure, it's still worth it. Failing is learning, which always leads to growing.

When you step into the role of coach, your value to the business multiplies. You're no longer the one producing the results; you're producing the people who produce the results. That's how you create scale, consistency, and longevity. And here's the most empowering part: When you embrace coaching as its own discipline, you start to see your team rise. They make better decisions. They solve more problems. They begin to lead. Suddenly, the business you once carried on your shoulders becomes something bigger: a shared vision powered by capable people. That's leadership. That's scalability. That's the difference between being the star of the show and being the one who built the stage.

Before I ever led a mortgage team, I was on the ice, not as a player, but as a referee in high-level hockey. At first glance, it might not seem like those years spent managing fast-paced, high-stakes games would have anything to do with business, but it turns out, refereeing taught me some of the most valuable leadership lessons I've ever learned. As a referee, you're not part of the play; you're overseeing it. You're managing chaos in real time, interpreting human behavior, and making split-second decisions with limited information. You have to anticipate problems before they boil over, stay composed under pressure, and command respect without controlling every move on the ice. In many ways, it's leadership at its rawest.

When I transitioned from refereeing to running a mortgage business, I was surprised by how much those lessons followed me into the office. Leading a mortgage team isn't about having all the answers. It's about knowing how to see the whole game. As a broker, when you're in the player role, you're chasing the puck, reacting to the next lead, the next deal, or the next deadline. But as a leader, your job shifts. You're not chasing the puck anymore. Instead, you're shaping the strategy. You're watching how the team moves, where the gaps are, and what systems need to be reinforced to keep things flowing smoothly.

At first, stepping off the ice (or out of the deal flow) can feel like you're giving up the fun part of the game. The adrenaline of winning the client, closing the file, solving the last-minute problem, that's what so many brokers thrive on after all. But once you fully commit to the coach's seat, you realize there's a new kind of fulfillment. You start winning differently. You see a team member solve a complex file because of the process you built. You watch a junior broker step into leadership because of the training you provided. You hear a client compliment your brand, not just you personally, and realize your business has a life beyond your individual effort.

That's the moment the shift clicks. You've gone from the ice to the office—from being in the game to shaping the game—and that's when you start building something that can outlast you.

Mindset That Builds a Business

As brokers evolve into leaders, one of the most important transitions is learning to recognize and respect the different mindsets that show up inside a business. Not everyone thinks like an owner…and they shouldn't. But understanding how these mindsets show up in your team is essential for scaling with intention. Over the years, I've observed three dominant mindsets in our industry: the Ownership Mindset, the Salesperson Mindset, and the Team Member Mindset. Each plays a critical role in a successful brokerage, but they're fundamentally different in how they view risk, responsibility, and reward. Let's take a closer look.

The Ownership Mindset

This is the mindset that builds a business, not just a book. People with an ownership mindset think long-term. They prioritize stability, structure, and sustainability. They're willing to take risks, delay gratification, and make decisions that may not benefit them today but strengthen the business for tomorrow. You'll notice this mindset in those who:

- Put the health of the business ahead of personal production

- Build systems and processes that can scale

- Invest in leadership development and culture

- Innovate, evolve, and adjust to market shifts

- Attract and retain strong people, not just more people

- Think in terms of equity, value, and brand, and not just commissions

- Pay themselves last, if necessary, to ensure others are looked after

These are your future partners. Your succession candidates. The ones who turn a practice into a sellable asset.

The Salesperson Mindset

Some of your highest earners fall into this category. They're driven, focused, and essential to revenue, but they operate with a different lens. Salespeople tend to prioritize their own books of business. They're client-first, goal-oriented, and competitive. They often:

- Focus on their own production and earning potential

- Thrive on recognition and reward

- Mentor others when time allows, but not at the cost of deals

- Expect influence based on performance

- Are unclear about the operational costs that support their success

- May want ownership, but without the weight that comes with it

Salespeople are the engine, but without a mindset shift, they're rarely the right fit for leadership—at least not yet. That's not a shortcoming. It's just a different role.

The Team Member Mindset

Often overlooked, this mindset is the glue that holds brokerages together. These are your processors, assistants, operations leaders, and marketing support. They're not building personal books or chasing ownership; they're building careers inside the business. They typically:

- Crave structure, clarity, and consistent communication

- Value appreciation and opportunities for advancement

- Prefer stability over financial risk

- Invest energy in execution, not equity

- Thrive when they feel seen, supported, and trusted

When team members are empowered, acknowledged, and connected to a bigger mission, they can elevate the entire client experience and help the business scale with consistency.

So, why does this matter? Because misunderstanding these mindsets creates conflict, while respecting them creates clarity. As a leader, your role is to assign the right roles to the right people and build compensation models that reflect each mindset. You also have to communicate in a way that resonates with different motivators and identify who has the desire and capacity to grow into leadership or ownership.

Not every great broker wants to lead, not every employee wants shares, and not every top producer is cut out for strategic decision-making, but when each mindset is recognized, nurtured, and given the space to thrive? That's when real magic happens! Ownership-minded leaders create the vision. Salesperson-minded brokers drive the volume. Team-member-minded professionals ensure delivery. Together, they don't just grow a brokerage, but they build a brand, a culture, and a business that lasts.

Company Culture as a Growth Lever

As you evolve from player to coach, one of the most critical and often underestimated transitions is recognizing that culture is what holds your business together when you're not in the room. Sure, systems scale operations, but culture scales leadership. In the early days, culture is mostly absorbed. Your team watches how you speak to clients, how you treat underwriters, and how you handle stress, and they follow suit. But as your business grows and more is delegated, your personal presence no longer sets the tone. That's when culture needs to shift from being implicit to intentional—visible, repeatable, and reinforced at every level.

However, let me be clear, culture isn't about office perks, birthday cakes, or casual Fridays. Culture is the "this is how we do things here." It's how your team behaves under pressure, how they make decisions in your absence, and how well their actions align with your mission and values. In high-growth mortgage businesses, culture is not a soft concept; it's a strategic asset. A strong culture:

- Improves retention by giving people a sense of belonging and meaning

- Attracts top talent who resonate with your values and leadership style

- Reduces friction by setting clear expectations for communication and conduct

- Protects the client experience by reinforcing standards as you scale

- Increases saleability by ensuring continuity beyond any one person (including you)

One of the most effective ways to cultivate culture is through storytelling. Don't just set rules or expectations. Instead, explain the "why" behind them. Share the stories that shaped your values. Help your team see themselves in the larger narrative of the business. Culture isn't built in a day. It's created through daily choices, consistent modeling, and conscious reinforcement. But if you want a business that thrives without your constant oversight, you need to start building culture with intention today.

Learn From Those Who've Been There

One of the most pivotal shifts in my career didn't come from a course or a conference. It came from a mastermind table where eight brokers from across Canada met regularly to grow together. At the time, our businesses ranged from $30 million to $100 million in volume. We all had different markets, models, and team structures, but we shared one key trait: We weren't satisfied with staying still. That group wasn't about socializing or swapping surface-level tips. Instead, it was about challenging each other to think bigger, move faster, and lead better.

The results of the group spoke for themselves. Those same businesses are now in the $100 million to $500 million+ range, not because we had magic formulas, but because we had a sounding board. A support system. A circle of accountability that pushed us to make the hard decisions we might've avoided on our own. The truth is, you don't have to build the business alone. There's a reason elite athletes have coaches. There's a reason high performers surround themselves with peers who stretch their thinking. Coaching and collaboration aren't luxuries; they're force multipliers. They compress your learning curve and give you a perspective you simply can't get in isolation.

You may be the leader of your team, but that doesn't mean you should stop being led. The best leaders are lifelong learners. They ask better questions. They surround themselves with people who challenge their assumptions and expand their vision. They invest in the right rooms. Whether it's a mastermind group, a mentor, a coach, or even a peer you meet with monthly, be sure to seek out those who've been where you want to go. Borrow their wisdom. Avoid their mistakes. Be open to being coached, even as you step into coaching others. Because the truth is, leadership is a team sport too.

Don't Forget Where You Came From

No one builds a successful mortgage business alone. Every thriving brokerage is the result of years (sometimes decades) of risk, hard work, and contributions from people who believed in something before it was fully built. But as businesses grow, leadership evolves, and teams expand, it becomes easier to lose sight of the road that got you here. This goes both ways.

Leaders can forget the early days: the long nights, lean months, and messy middle stages. They may overlook the people who stood by them through instability, uncertainty, and inconsistent pay. These were the teammates who showed up before the brand was polished and before the revenue was predictable. On the other hand, team members, especially those who join later, may not realize what came before. They step into structure, culture, and opportunity without always seeing the history behind it. It's easy to focus on today's KPIs, compensation plans, or leadership decisions without understanding the weight of what it took to make those things possible.

As a leader, one of your responsibilities is to keep that origin story alive. Not for vanity. Not to romanticize the past. But to ground the business in perspective. How? By sharing the milestones, talking about the challenges, and celebrating the people who helped shape the early days, and the ones who stayed through transition and change. Doing so reinforces a culture of respect. It reminds newer team members that they're part of something bigger, and it helps long-time contributors feel seen and valued, even as the business evolves.

The strongest leadership transitions are built not just on systems and structures, but on a shared understanding of where the business began and a collective commitment to where it's headed.

So, never forget where you came from. It's one of the most powerful ways to build trust as you grow.

Leadership Is a Choice

Let's be clear: not every broker needs to become a leader. Some choose to stay in the lane of high-performing producers, doing what they love: closing deals, serving clients, and staying in the action. That's a valid path. In fact, it can be a very lucrative and fulfilling one. But if your goal is to scale, build a legacy, or create something sellable, then leadership isn't optional. The hard truth is that scaling a business means scaling yourself out of the day-to-day. It means shifting from being the one who does it all to the one who builds the people and systems that do it all. That's the difference between a career and a company, between a job and an asset. It's no joke, and it's not easy.

You'll make mistakes. You'll hire the wrong person. You'll over-train one team member and under-delegate to another. You'll swing between micromanaging and letting go too fast. It will feel awkward—especially if you're used to being the top producer, the rainmaker, the one who always has the answer—but leadership takes time because it's a skill you need to acquire. Like every skill in brokering, it can be learned, refined, and mastered with practice. No one becomes a great coach overnight. You learn through repetition, trial, and error. Through investing in your own growth, you can better support the growth of others. You don't need to have all the answers at once, but you do need to choose to step up.

You have to be okay with letting your team make mistakes; it's all part of the growing process. Sure, by delegating responsibilities and growing your team, your profitability might decrease, but only until the system is running smoothly. Then, you'll have more capacity for clients, which means more revenue. Don't consider a dip in revenue a loss of profit, but see it as building for the long term. It's an investment in the future of your business. Even when profit drops for a short period of time, eventually it will be worth it.

Leadership isn't about a title. It's about ownership. It's about owning the vision, the direction, and the responsibility of building something bigger than yourself. So pause for a moment and ask yourself: Do you want to just produce or do you want to build? Do you want to stay in the game or shape it? Either choice is valid, but only one leads to scale, and if you've made it this far in the book, I have a feeling you're ready to lead or have the insight to hire a great coach.

Free Download: Leadership Self-Assessment Quiz

For a free downloadable self-assessment to evaluate your leadership strengths and identify areas for growth, go to: dougadlam.com/brokering

Or scan the QR code below:

Chapter 9

Stop, Start, Continue— Feedback as a Growth Tool

We've spoken a lot about growth so far. We've looked at various ways to grow your brokerage into something sellable. But there's one element of growth that often flies under the radar. It's not something you can buy or something you can delegate. It's not something that occurs naturally or by accident. It's something you need to build into your structure from the get-go. What is it? Feedback. I know, it doesn't sound very important or very glamorous, but good feedback can make your business, and a lack thereof can be your downfall. Real, honest, structured feedback can be more valuable than rates, leads, and lender relationships. Yet very few brokers take the time to pause and ask the most powerful questions in business: What's working? What's not? What's missing?

This is where the "Stop, Start, Continue" framework enters. It's a deceptively simple yet highly effective tool that turns vague observations into actionable growth steps. It's not about critique for critique's sake. It's about clarity, alignment, and continuous improvement. Whether you're leading a team, mentoring an associate, or just reflecting on your business habits, this framework helps you zoom out, examine what needs to change, and course correct with purpose. The key to feedback lies in knowing that you won't get it all right the first time. If you believe you can't do anything wrong, you won't see the need for feedback. But when you realize that there's always a place to grow and learn, you'll welcome feedback with open arms.

In this chapter, we'll explore how feedback can become a competitive advantage when it's structured, consistent, and welcomed. You'll learn why real feedback is so rare, how to give and receive it without defensiveness, and how to turn it into a ritual that fuels both personal and team growth. The truth is, you can't scale what you don't inspect, and you can't grow what you don't question. So, let's stop guessing and start listening. Let's continue to build businesses that improve with every cycle of feedback.

A Brief History Lesson

The "Stop, Start, Continue" feedback model originated in the world of organizational development and strategic consulting. It was first introduced by Phil Daniels and colleagues at McKinsey & Company as a way to streamline performance conversations and remove the guesswork from improvement strategies. At its core, the model was built to simplify feedback. The goal was to make feedback more specific, actionable, and less confrontational. Instead of vague suggestions or general praise, this model encourages people to look at behaviors and systems through three simple lenses:

- What should we stop doing because it's no longer serving us?

- What should we start doing to improve or grow?

- What should we continue doing because it's working well?

This structure makes it easier to give and receive feedback without defensiveness. It takes the sting out of performance reviews and replaces it with curiosity and collaboration. Over time, the model has spread beyond consulting circles and it's now widely used in schools, startups, boardrooms, and service-based industries, including mortgage brokering.

This model serves our industry well as it focuses on speed, clarity, and adaptability. In a business where things move fast and client experience is everything, this model offers a way to hit pause and assess performance, ultimately helping us to grow intentionally. For brokers, team leads, and even solo operators, this model provides a repeatable rhythm for genuine reflection, eliminating any unnecessary fluff and corporate jargon.

Why Real Feedback is Rare and Valuable

In many brokerages, feedback only shows up when something goes wrong. When a deal falls through, a team member drops the ball, or a client complains, feedback is suddenly resurrected, dusted off, and used as a tool to "get to the bottom" of the issue. In that reactive model, feedback becomes a tool for correction and not a driver of growth. No wonder most people are so scared of the word "feedback." It has been used for many years and across numerous industries as a corrective tool, driven by fear and failure. Within that mindset, feedback is often limited and can have a profound impact on the morale of your organization.

The most effective leaders treat feedback not as a once-in-a-while fix, but as a constant, strategic lever. Done right, feedback isn't just about course correction, but about acceleration. It's how you unlock insight, improve systems, and sharpen your edge before issues even arise. Here's the challenge: Most brokers operate in a kind of professional echo chamber. If you're a solo agent, you may be moving quickly and executing well, but without outside input, your blind spots stay hidden. If you're leading a team, there's often a power dynamic that prevents honest conversations. It's natural for people to hesitate to "call out the boss," even when they have valuable perspectives.

Over time, this lack of feedback creates a ceiling. You keep working harder, but you're not necessarily working smarter. Without regular, structured reflection, growth becomes accidental rather than intentional. That's what makes real feedback so rare, but so valuable. It takes intention to build a culture where honest input is welcomed and acted on. It takes intention to stop viewing feedback as a weapon that breaks down and see it as a tool that can help build. But once you do it, it becomes one of the most powerful accelerators in your business.

The Framework: Stop, Start, Continue

At its core, the "Stop, Start, Continue" framework is a straightforward yet powerful structure for generating clear and actionable feedback. It removes ambiguity, encourages reflection, and helps you focus on what really matters in your business. We already know that it adopts the idea of looking at your business through three lenses, but let's take a closer look at each lens as we begin to explore the kind of business we're building or want to build.

Stop

The first step is to stop and ask yourself, "What is no longer serving my business?" This could be a process that creates bottlenecks, a habit that drains your energy, or even a belief that limits your growth. Think about outdated systems, micromanagement tendencies, unnecessary meetings, or marketing strategies that no longer perform. Identifying what to stop is about clearing the runway for better things to take off. Here's the key to success, though: Sometimes the things you need to stop are the very things that helped you to get where you are. For example, if you've used your face and name to build your business, great! It's gotten you this far. But now you might want to stop focusing so much attention on your image as you're building something sellable. The thing you have to stop isn't necessarily an inherently bad thing, but it's something "bad" for your business in the specific season you find yourself in.

Start

Next, you need to ask yourself the question, "What should I be doing that I'm not doing right now?" These are the new actions, systems, or mindsets that will improve performance. Most of us have that list in our mind that we know we should be paying attention to, or those things we want to implement, but we haven't had the time to do so. Well, the time is now. No more procrastinating or focusing on other things instead. Maybe it's implementing a new CRM, tracking KPIs more consistently, or having regular one-on-ones with your team. Starting isn't just about doing more. It's also about doing things in a smarter way. Starting something new might seem daunting, but it can be the very thing that saves you more time and energy (and perhaps even money) in the near future.

Continue

The last element of this model is to ask yourself, "What is working well and deserves more attention?" So often, we overlook the importance of celebrating the elements of our business that are working well. It's doing its job, so we don't have to focus on that, right? Well, not really. If you don't acknowledge which systems are working and which ones aren't, you might end up wanting to pause or change the aspects that are working. During "continue," you look at the strengths you want to maintain and amplify. It might be client touchpoints that build loyalty, the workflow that runs smoothly, or the team dynamics that foster trust. Identifying your "continue" items reinforces what's been driving results and keeps morale high.

What I love about this framework is the fact that it's versatile. It's not limited to self-reflection! You don't have to identify all of these elements on your own because you might have blind spots you're missing. You can apply this model across nearly every area of your business. For example:

- **Client experience:** What's frustrating clients that need to stop? What could enhance their journey that you should start? What parts of the process do they love that you should continue?

- **Team development:** What leadership behavior or team habits are dragging you down? What training, recognition, or routines are missing? What team dynamics are working and should be protected?

- **Marketing:** What campaigns are underperforming? What platforms or messages should be explored? What brand assets are consistently resonating?

- **Technology:** What tools are clunky or outdated? What new tech could streamline operations? What systems are quietly saving you time?

The beauty of "Stop, Start, Continue" is that it's flexible. You can use it quarterly, after every major campaign, after a bad month, or after a great month! Whether you're reflecting solo or running team sessions, this framework will keep you grounded in clarity and forward motion, which is a win in itself.

Frequency and Implementation

We now know that this model can be valuable, but here's the catch: The "Stop, Start, Continue" framework is only as valuable as its frequency and follow-through. While many businesses treat feedback like an annual obligation, in fast-moving industries like mortgage brokering, once a year simply isn't enough. In today's Canadian real estate and finance landscape, a lot can change in 90 days. Lender policies can shift, economic fluctuations take place, regulatory updates happen, and even client behaviors can all pivot within a single quarter. That's why quarterly implementation of this feedback model is an ideal minimum. To gain the full value of the "Stop, Start, Continue" framework, it needs to occur at three distinct levels:

Individual Broker Level

Each broker should evaluate their own habits, tools, and mindset. What's holding them back? What new approaches could elevate their workflow? What's driving consistent success? A quarterly self-assessment can foster personal ownership and agile growth. When you don't assess yourself often, blind spots have the tendency to grow bigger and bigger. While you can't see everything from a personal point of view, you can dig deep into your own mind and actions, enabling you to determine whether your goals are still aligned with your actions and whether you are truly happy with what you've built. The thing is, we all change. As we grow and enter new seasons of our lives, our goals and values might change. That's why we need to self-assess regularly and not just once every five years.

Team Level

This is where collaboration, culture, and operational friction come into focus. Maybe one team member is duplicating efforts already being handled elsewhere. Or maybe a process isn't working as smoothly as it seemed at the beginning. These are all things that can be identified and worked on during quarterly team-based feedback meetings. These meetings will help eliminate team blind spots, surface innovation, and strengthen collaboration. This isn't a "let's share what bothers us about someone else" session. These meetings are constructive and uplifting, aimed at propelling the business and team forward. It's vital to set guidelines for feedback meetings like these and to keep the team on track with "Stop, Start, Continue" chats to prevent it from spiraling into a massive, unconstructive venting session.

Leadership Level

At the leadership table, "Stop, Start, Continue" becomes a tool for shaping the strategic direction of the business. It's a space to ask: What operational inefficiencies need to stop? What new tech, training, or positioning do we need to start? What leadership behaviors and business functions are clearly working and should be scaled? Having chats like these at the leadership table can transform the way you run your business. It also ensures that everyone is aligned. Gone are the days when one partner might think an element of the business is working while another knows that it's not. Alignment and agreement on the next steps are vital, especially if you're growing a business into something sellable.

If quarterly sounds too frequent at first, consider this: In brokering, waiting too long to adapt often costs more than moving quickly. Semi-annual reviews might catch issues eventually, but by then, you may have already lost market share, talent, or efficiency. Feedback isn't just about solving problems, but also about staying ahead of them. One of the most powerful outcomes of this rhythm is pattern recognition. Issues that once seemed isolated become visible as a trend. When feedback is collected and reviewed quarterly, you start to see recurring signals: the same delay, the same communication gap, and the same missed opportunities. This is where the real growth begins, not from reacting to one-offs, but from proactively spotting and addressing themes.

Back in my early career as a market research analyst, one of the most valuable lessons I learned was how to distinguish between statistical outliers (random, often irrelevant anomalies) and trends (emerging patterns that signal something meaningful). The same principle applies here: Don't get distracted by the occasional complaint or one-time fluke. Focus on consistent feedback. That's where your leverage is. This quarterly cadence doesn't just create a rhythm, but it builds a culture. A culture where clarity is valued and continuous improvement and ownership occur. When your team knows that feedback isn't a one-time event but a consistent practice, they begin to trust it, and that's where transformation starts.

Making Feedback a Ritual

A framework only becomes really powerful when it becomes habitual. To unlock the full potential of "Stop, Start, Continue," it needs to evolve from a one-time exercise into a business ritual. You already know that it's suggested to use this framework at least quarterly, but here's how you can make it part of a ritual or business habit. Let's be honest, you might have all the intention to implement this framework, but without a plan, we both know it's not likely to happen. Here's how you can make it happen:

- **Schedule it:** Don't leave feedback to chance or emotion or for when something goes wrong. Decide how often you want feedback sessions and schedule them into the calendar. Whether it's feedback with yourself, with the team, or with other stakeholders, schedule it! Set aside time to review, discuss, and document your insights and treat it with the same importance as lender updates or client strategy meetings, because it's just as critical to the success of your business.

- **Tie feedback to real data:** Make your feedback meaningful by anchoring it in evidence. Look at CRM reports, response times, conversion rates, client reviews, lender feedback, and file completion metrics. When feedback is connected to actual performance indicators, it moves from opinions to insights. This also reduces defensiveness since you're not going on guesswork but on measures.

- **Use it to adjust your plan:** Feedback should never exist in a vacuum. Once you've identified what to stop, start, and continue, schedule time to take action. Let the results inform your quarterly goals, marketing strategy, hiring decisions, or client experience updates. The point of feedback isn't analysis; it's alignment. What you learn should translate directly into your business roadmap.

- **Make it collaborative:** If you lead a team, don't just make this a leadership exercise. Bring everyone into the room, including senior brokers, junior brokers, underwriters, assistants, and even marketing and admin team members. You'll be surprised by what they see. Often, they're the closest to the client pain points, the system hiccups, or the culture wins that leadership overlooks. Giving them a voice builds trust and makes your business smarter.

When feedback becomes a ritual, performance becomes proactive. Instead of waiting for problems to escalate or opportunities to pass you by, you begin to spot shifts early. Your team starts thinking like owners, and you will begin to build a culture where people aren't afraid of feedback, but look forward to it. That's when momentum kicks in and can carry you forward. However, remember that feedback isn't about becoming perfect, but about staying in tune, on track, and ahead of the curve.

Feedback in Action

One of the most valuable insights we've ever received as a brokerage didn't come from a marketing report or internal review. It came directly from client feedback. Over time, a recurring theme began to emerge: Clients were unclear about the mortgage process, especially around when and how they were expected to formally commit to working with a broker. While we were focused on securing a yes—a verbal commitment or a submitted application—many clients were still uncertain about what that commitment actually meant. The truth? We were asking for clarity and loyalty from our clients, without first providing it ourselves.

Some clients believed they were required to wait until they had signed legal documents before selecting their broker. Others believed a mortgage approval was still non-binding and that they could continue to shop around, even after we had done the heavy lifting. That ambiguity created friction and anxiety, not just for us as brokers, but for the clients as well. They were unsure when the real relationship started, and what it meant once it did. So, we looked inward and here's what we realized: If we wanted loyalty, clarity, and commitment from clients, we needed to lead the way.

That's when we introduced a formal Agreement of Understanding as discussed in earlier chapters. This wasn't a contract in the legal sense, but a communication tool. It was a document designed to clearly outline when the professional relationship officially begins, what clients can expect from us throughout the process, what we require in return once a commitment is made, and what exclusive representation entails in a mortgage transaction. We used it to educate, set expectations, and give clients the confidence they needed to move forward. It removed the pressure of uncertainty and replaced it with a shared understanding. In doing so, we weren't just protecting our time and effort; we were delivering a better, more transparent experience.

This single adjustment had a massive ripple effect on our business. Firstly, it meant that we had fewer last-minute deal losses. Before, clients would sometimes walk away late in the game, lured by gimmicks like cashback offers from competitors. Now, with the agreement in place, we could point back to a mutual understanding, and the client felt accountable to the process they'd committed to.

Secondly, we experienced higher trust and smoother closings in general. With clearer roles and expectations, clients stopped second-guessing the process. They stopped shopping mid-deal because they understood what it meant to engage a broker professionally and that we had already delivered on our end. Lastly, it improved our industry relationships. Lenders noticed the change! When brokers submit cleaner, more committed files, lenders face fewer abandoned deals and last-minute changes. That efficiency matters. It reduces costs, builds trust, and enables lenders to focus their resources where they have the most impact: on faster approvals, better rates, and innovation that benefits all.

All of this came from listening and acting on feedback. What started as client confusion became a catalyst for one of the most significant and effective changes we had made to our process. It's proof that feedback isn't just reactive, but transformative. When you treat it not as criticism but as insight, it becomes strategic—something you can put into action. You don't need a massive overhaul to improve your business. Sometimes, the most powerful growth comes from small, intentional changes that directly address what your clients are already telling you. The key is to listen and then lead.

Personal Examples

The "Stop, Start, Continue" framework is more than just a coaching tool. It's something that you should apply to every aspect of your business. Real feedback from our teams and clients has led to some of the most pivotal improvements we've made. Here are some examples of how this model played out for us in practice:

Stop: Micromanaging Team Processes

One of the most revealing pieces of feedback I received from our team was that I was inadvertently creating drag. My intention was good: I wanted visibility, consistency, and follow-through. But in practice, my habit of double-checking deals and following up on nearly every task created bottlenecks. I had essentially "CRM'd" the team to death. We had built an incredibly detailed task management system where every milestone, every handoff, and every follow-up was automated. From an operational standpoint, it looked impressive. But the feedback was clear: It was too much. Team members felt overburdened by the volume of tasks and overwhelmed by notifications that didn't always align with their natural workflow. We were creating friction in the name of control.

The lesson? Structure is only valuable if it supports autonomy. So, we took a step back. We audited our workflows, reduced the number of automated tasks, and gave team members the flexibility to adapt the process to their working style, as long as the outcomes and milestones were still met. The result was powerful: improved morale, more trust, and a smoother internal flow. We didn't lower our standards; we just removed unnecessary friction.

Start: Implementing Structured Quarterly Reviews

For a long time, we assumed we were communicating well. We held meetings. We sent Google messages. We shared wins. But beneath the surface, frustrations were building, and we weren't catching them early enough. It was during a team feedback session that someone said, "I don't feel like there's a place to raise concerns unless they're urgent." That stuck with me. So, we started holding structured quarterly reviews, not just for performance, but for open dialogue. Brokers and admin teams were given a chance to reflect on what was working, what wasn't, and what they needed from leadership and each other. The tone was collaborative, not corrective.

Within a single cycle, we identified misalignments in capacity planning, client communication handoffs, and support coverage during vacation periods, all of which were negatively impacting the client experience. None of these issues was significant individually, but left unchecked, they were eroding efficiency and morale. By creating space for honest conversations, we built a culture where feedback felt safe and useful. Small course corrections became possible before big problems developed.

Continue: Tuesday and Thursday Huddles

One of the best decisions we made was introducing twice-weekly huddles. These quick, 30-minute meetings brought brokers, underwriters, and support staff together to align on deals in progress, surface blockers, and celebrate quick wins. Over time, the rhythm took hold, and we noticed something unexpected. These huddles were doing more than improving workflow; they were strengthening culture. They fostered trust, speed, and a sense of shared ownership. Eventually, many teams added daily 15-minute huddles, customized by function or deal stage. Brokers and their assistants could connect quickly each morning, clarify priorities, and avoid the delays caused by endless back-and-forth emails. The compounding effect was enormous:

- Faster decision-making

- Fewer dropped balls

- Stronger team cohesion

This simple ritual, inspired by practices employed at Apple and other high-performing organizations, remains one of the highest return-on-investment (ROI) leadership tools in our business. It doesn't cost a cent, but it pays dividends in alignment, accountability, and culture.

Each of these shifts (stopping micromanagement, starting structured reviews, continuing short-form communication) came directly from feedback. Not from a book, not from a Ted Talk, but from the people doing the work every day. That's the power of "Stop, Start, Continue." It meets you where you are and points you toward where you could be—if you're willing to listen.

Client Feedback

In the mortgage industry, we've developed a bit of a blind spot when it comes to client feedback. We often treat Google reviews and other public-facing testimonials as the gold standard. And yes, they're valuable—they build trust with future clients and support our marketing efforts—but they're also curated. Clients are far more likely to leave glowing public reviews than to share the awkward moment when something didn't land. They don't want to damage a relationship, and they often don't feel comfortable pointing out where things fell short, especially as they still have a mortgage. That's why real, constructive client feedback is rare and incredibly valuable. It reveals what no testimonial ever will: the missed expectations, confusing steps, or small frictions that could cost you referrals and loyalty in the long run.

That's why we introduced what we called "Post-Closing Feedback." When we first introduced it, it was fairly straightforward. Brokers would reach out after closing to check in and ask how the process went. However, we soon noticed a pattern: The feedback was almost always positive, yet generic. Clients would say things like, "Everything was great!" or "You were so helpful!" These things are nice to hear, but not useful. We realized that when brokers ran the follow-up themselves, clients rarely gave honest, critical feedback. Even when they had suggestions or concerns, they didn't want to hurt the broker's feelings. It was a classic case of feedback being filtered by politeness.

So, we changed the process. I started making the follow-up calls myself. I wasn't their broker; I was someone asking on behalf of the business, with a genuine interest in improving the experience. And I didn't just ask, "How did it go?" I asked:

- "Was there a moment when you felt confused, uncertain, or in the dark?"

- "Did anything happen that made you question whether you'd made the right choice?"

- "Was there something we could have done sooner, faster, or better?"

Those questions opened up real conversations. Clients shared when they felt rushed, unclear about what came next, or unsure when their commitment actually began. These were things we never would have learned through a five-star review. Eventually, we refined the process again. We designated one support team member to conduct all post-closing follow-ups across the brokerage. This created consistency and psychological safety. Suddenly, clients were more comfortable giving honest feedback when the conversation felt neutral, not personal.

We didn't just collect the responses and wag our finger at anything done "wrong." Instead, we started creating a culture of curiosity and improvement. If three different clients mentioned confusion about document collection timelines, we didn't blame the broker; we adjusted the communication templates. Over time, this process became one of our most excellent growth tools. It provided us with clear insights into how our service was being experienced, opportunities to refine workflows and communication, greater alignment across brokers, underwriters, and administrative staff, and a culture where feedback was normalized and valued.

The takeaway? If you're not proactively asking for and acting on client feedback, you're leaving growth on the table. Marketing is what gets people in the door. Client feedback is what keeps them coming back.

The Contribution Gap

One of the most common and quietly destructive tensions inside growing broker businesses is what I call the Contribution Gap: the disconnect between perceived value and recognized reward. And it's almost always two-sided. On one hand, you have leaders who unintentionally overlook or underappreciate meaningful contributions, especially the ones that don't show up in a P&L. On the other, you have team members who overestimate the impact of their work, expecting rewards that may not align with actual business outcomes.

It's a breeding ground for friction: resentment, entitlement, miscommunication, and sometimes even exits. There's no universal formula for who deserves what, but there is a powerful tool: open, consistent feedback. That's exactly where Stop, Start, Continue comes in. This simple framework creates space for proactive dialogue. It helps leaders acknowledge meaningful contributions before frustration festers, and it helps team members understand how their work is being viewed through a business lens, not just through effort or intention.

When someone goes above and beyond, say so. Celebrate it. That doesn't always mean cutting a cheque. It might mean a handwritten note, public praise, or a meaningful conversation. But it should be thoughtful, timely, and sincere. When contributions do meet a threshold for financial recognition or expanded responsibility, make the criteria clear and consistent. For example:

- Sales performance might trigger commission-based bonuses.

- Process improvements might lead to a one-time bonus or a new leadership opportunity.

- Team culture contributions might be recognized with personal appreciation or extra time off.

- Curiosity and creativity may lead to additional professional development opportunities.

The key is alignment between contribution, recognition, and expectation. Most day-to-day contributions, especially from your support team, can be acknowledged through micro-rewards: thank-you notes, lunch on the house, or shout-outs in team meetings. But when someone believes they've made a game-changing impact, and leadership doesn't recognize it, or worse, isn't even aware, the Contribution Gap widens.

So, don't wait for tension to build. Use Stop, Start, Continue to close the loop early. Normalize open conversations about value, impact, and reward. The best-run brokerages don't just hand out trophies; they build a culture where contribution is seen, celebrated, and understood. That's how you retain your best people, reduce unnecessary conflict, and stay focused on the bigger picture.

Building The Feedback Loop

In our tech venture, we didn't stumble into innovation; we engineered it. From day one, we designed a feedback loop that was intentional, responsive, and tightly woven into the core of our business strategy. Why? Because we weren't just trying to build a product. We were trying to build something people loved—not only because it worked, but because they felt heard. We embedded multiple channels for user feedback directly into the experience, such as in-app messaging for real-time reactions, email follow-ups for deeper insights, and prompted surveys to capture suggestions, frustrations, and wish lists.

This wasn't a passive inbox exercise. Every piece of feedback, big or small, was reviewed weekly and categorized for action. Then, during our sprint planning meetings, that feedback directly shaped our development priorities. The result? We pushed live product updates every single week. Not once a quarter. Not twice a year. Every. Week. That's what it looks like when feedback isn't treated as a box to check, but as a driver of innovation, trust, and loyalty. The lesson applies just as powerfully in mortgage brokering as it does in tech. Whether you're managing a team, serving clients, or building systems, feedback isn't something you react to, but rather something you build around. The more embedded it becomes in your operations, the more resilient and responsive your business becomes.

So, build the loop. Make feedback a system, not a surprise. Make it part of your culture, part of your sprints, your huddles, your reviews, and your one-on-ones. Make it safe, make it regular, and most of all, act on it. In a fast-moving business, the people who grow the fastest are those who listen best.

Free Download: Feedback Templates

For a free downloadable set of templates to collect and implement feedback from your team and clients, go to: dougadlam.com/brokering

Or scan the QR code below:

Chapter 10

Client Experience is a Business Asset

In the mortgage business, it's easy to reduce client experience to a buzzword. You know, something talked about in marketing meetings and plastered on websites. But when done right, client experience becomes much more than that. It becomes a competitive advantage, a retention tool, and ultimately, a tangible business asset. Some businesses invest in a done-for-you CRM or marketing automation platform and consider their work done. But true client experience design goes far deeper. It begins with understanding the entire mortgage journey, from initial interaction and discovery to funding and follow-up, and optimizing every touchpoint to minimize friction, foster trust, and provide clarity.

In an industry filled with complex paperwork, strict regulations, and overwhelming decisions, brokers who prioritize simplicity and emotional intelligence set themselves apart. A well-designed client experience doesn't just help you close more deals; it creates loyalty, drives referrals, and elevates your brand beyond rates and products. This chapter examines the concept of intentionally designing a mortgage business with the customer at its center.

We'll dive into the importance of user-first technology, how to simplify the mortgage journey for modern consumers, and how to operationalize your client experience in a way that supports sustainable growth. Most importantly, you'll learn how a consistent, thoughtful client experience becomes a brand asset. Let's unpack how delivering an outstanding client experience isn't just good service but a smart strategy.

Customer-First Product Design

When we co-founded a mortgage technology company, our north star was clear: build a platform that served the borrower first, not just the broker. It was a bold idea at the time. The mortgage industry had long treated technology as a back-office tool, focused on broker workflows and internal efficiencies. Borrowers were often an afterthought, expected to adapt to clunky processes and opaque systems. We set out to change that. Every feature we designed had to enhance the client experience. We asked ourselves tough, practical questions:

- Where do borrowers feel confused or overwhelmed?

- What steps in the process create unnecessary friction?

- How can we make compliance and documentation feel seamless rather than intrusive?

- Where do clients typically get stuck, hesitate, or drop off entirely?

- What are the common questions that stop a borrower in their tracks?

This user-first mindset didn't just lead to a better product; it also accelerated adoption. Brokers embraced our technology not just because of the functionality it gave them, but because their clients found it intuitive, clear, and refreshingly human. The result? Faster applications, higher-quality data, and smoother documentation collection, all of which allowed brokers to better understand and serve their clients.

But here's the real disruption: We built a platform in which the borrower was the primary user. The broker paid for it, but the borrower's experience came first. That single design choice, flipping the traditional hierarchy on its head, changed everything. We weren't just improving a tool; we were reimagining how the entire industry could operate. Of course, challenging the status quo isn't easy. It takes conviction to swim against the current, to ask "Why is it done this way?" and "Could it be better?" But that's where real innovation begins. It's not enough to build what's expected. Progress means having the courage to question deeply held assumptions and design with empathy, not just efficiency.

The lesson here is universal: Whether you're designing a piece of software, a customer journey, or an internal process, start with the user. Make their experience your priority. When you do, adoption increases, loyalty strengthens, and you build something that isn't just functional, but transformational.

A Thriving Tech Landscape

Competition breeds innovation, and nowhere is that more evident than in the mortgage technology space. While I firmly believe Finmo was a true disruptor in introducing a borrower-first experience, I'm equally encouraged by the robust and diverse ecosystem of platforms that now serve our industry. What we're seeing is not just a wave of new tools, but a complete shift in mindset: Technology is no longer a nice-to-have; it's foundational to how modern brokerages operate and scale.

As previously mentioned, back when I started in 2008, the landscape was virtually monopolized. You had Filogix Expert with over 99% market share, and Marlborough Stirling holding the tiniest sliver of the market. Innovation was slow, options were limited, and user experience was not prioritized. Brokers were forced to adapt to the system, not the other way around. Fast forward to today, and the picture couldn't be more different.

You now have Velocity pushing the pace with aggressive updates and a vision for modernization. Scarlett is carving out its niche with clean design and thoughtful UX. Boss continues to reinvent itself with increased flexibility and automation tools. Hurricane by Unison is steadily gaining traction with a focus on customizable workflows and borrower engagement. And Filogix, now bolstered by its acquisition of Doorr, is working to stay relevant through its Filogix 2.0 platform. The result? Brokers have real choice, and with choice comes empowerment. You no longer have to settle for a system that doesn't serve your team or your clients.

You can evaluate platforms based on how they align with your values, your workflow, and most importantly, your client experience. More importantly, this competitive environment keeps every player on their toes. When one platform introduces a new feature that improves borrower transparency or speeds up the approval process, others are forced to respond. It creates a feedback loop of innovation, which benefits the entire ecosystem.

But this isn't just about shiny new tools. This is about building a better business. When tech works for you, when it's intuitive, responsive, and designed with the client in mind, it frees you to focus on relationships, strategy, and growth. It creates space for your team to spend less time clicking and more time connecting. This vibrant tech landscape also creates pressure for ongoing professional development. As new systems emerge and existing ones evolve, brokers must invest in learning and adaptation. Staying static is no longer an option; not if you want to remain competitive. The brokers who thrive are the ones who embrace new tools early, experiment with them, and integrate them into their processes with intention.

In short, the playing field has never been more dynamic, and that's a good thing. The bar for client experience is rising, and with it, so are the expectations for what it means to be a truly modern mortgage professional. The technology you choose is no longer just about efficiency, but a reflection of your brand, your values, and your commitment to delivering an exceptional client journey.

Simplifying the Mortgage Journey

On a recent podcast, we talked about something that's easy for mortgage professionals to forget: Most borrowers only go through this process a handful of times in their lives. To us, it's routine. To them, it's unfamiliar, emotionally charged, and often overwhelming. It's not second nature; it's stressful. And that's precisely why they're relying on us not just for execution, but for clarity, confidence, and reassurance. Yet far too often, our processes are built for our own convenience, not theirs.

We optimize workflows to fit our internal operations. We send jargon-heavy emails that make sense to lenders and underwriters, but leave clients confused. We pass files between departments or team members with minimal explanation, leaving borrowers wondering who's who and what's happening next.

Now, imagine flipping that approach completely. What if your onboarding emails weren't just automated, but friendly, personal, and laser-focused on reducing anxiety? What if you used short explainer videos to walk through complex documents, anticipating the very questions borrowers might be too embarrassed to ask? What if your CRM wasn't just a checklist of tasks, but a journey map built around client emotions, from excitement and relief to fear and hesitation? Every touchpoint is an opportunity to either create friction or build trust. Every message, form, or conversation either brings a client closer to feeling supported or pushes them further into doubt.

Simplifying the journey doesn't mean dumbing it down. It means removing unnecessary complexity. It means anticipating confusion and proactively resolving it. It means delivering information in ways people can absorb, and not just what's technically accurate, but also what's emotionally reassuring. Think about the times you've booked a flight, ordered takeout, or opened a bank account. When the company walked you through each step clearly, you barely noticed how smooth it was. That's the goal: a seamless, stress-free path where the client always knows what's happening, what's expected, and what's next. In fact, simplification is one of the most powerful forms of differentiation.

In a market where rates, lenders, and products may look similar from the outside, the experience becomes the deciding factor. If you're the broker who made things feel easy, who turned a confusing process into a guided journey, you'll be the one they remember, recommend, and return to because, ultimately, the mortgage journey isn't about the transaction; it's about how the client feels throughout it. When you simplify with empathy, you don't just close deals; you also build lasting relationships.

Experience as a Growth Engine

The most successful brokers in the country aren't just closing more deals; they're delivering a better experience, and doing it consistently. That consistency is the secret ingredient behind sustainable, organic growth. It fuels glowing testimonials, enthusiastic referrals, and repeat business that doesn't require constant chasing. In short, experience becomes your engine, quietly but powerfully driving your business forward.

Unlike interest rates or lender policies, both of which are constantly changing and beyond your control, your client experience is something you own completely. It's yours to shape, refine, and scale. And that makes it one of the most defensible assets in your business. But let's be clear: Great experiences don't happen by accident. They're built through intentional systems, and consistency is what turns those systems into something sellable.

One of the biggest mistakes business owners make is breaking their own process. It happens innocently enough. A long-time client asks for something "a little different." A family member gets special treatment.

A top referral partner wants things done a certain way. You think, "It's just this once." But over time, those exceptions become the norm, and suddenly your process is no longer predictable. Your team doesn't know what to expect, your clients don't get a consistent experience, and your results start to drift.

The thing is, you've built your process for a reason. Every step was put in place to ensure efficiency, quality, and client clarity. Every deviation from that process introduces risk to the timeline, to the experience, and ultimately to your brand. A consistent, replicable process doesn't mean robotic. It means reliable. It means every client gets the same thoughtful, professional treatment, whether they're a first-time buyer or a seasoned investor. It means your team can deliver with confidence because they know the playbook. It means your business becomes something you can delegate without dilution, where quality doesn't depend solely on you.

This is especially important if you're thinking long-term, such as growing a team, stepping out of day-to-day operations, or eventually selling your business. Consistency is what turns your client experience into a repeatable asset and something that adds measurable value to the company. Remember, people don't refer companies. They refer experiences. They say, "You've got to talk to my broker! They made everything so clear and simple." Or, "It was the smoothest transaction I've ever had." That doesn't happen by luck. It happens when you've deliberately designed and protected your client journey.

So, build it with intention. Document your process, train your team on it, resist the temptation to make too many exceptions, and commit to delivering the same high-level experience every single time. Because the more predictable your experience becomes, the more powerful your brand becomes and the more your business grows, without having to push so hard to make it happen.

Your Client Experience is Your Brand

At its core, your client experience is your brand, not just the colours in your logo or the tagline on your website. It's the emotional imprint you leave. It's how people feel when they work with your company. And that feeling carries remarkable power. Think back to your own experiences. You likely remember more how a company made you feel than what they claimed about themselves. Maybe it was the reassurance of a helpful email, the surprise of lightning-fast approval, or the simplicity of a video walkthrough. That's brand. That's trust. That's what makes your business feel real and memorable.

Over the years, I've spent countless hours obsessing over this journey, first as a mortgage broker and later as a fintech founder. In every role, one truth stood clear: No matter how good you are, there's always room for refinement. Innovation isn't a luxury; it's essential. You've probably heard the phrase, "If you're not growing, you're dying." The same holds true for experience and innovation. If you're not updating, improving, and optimizing your client journey, your competitors will. So, here's what I recommend:

- **Create a journey:** Don't leave the client experience to chance. Map it out. Consider how people feel at every stage, and design accordingly.

- **Stick to the process:** Consistency builds trust. Protect your systems, they're the foundation of your brand.

- **Continuously improve:** Treat your client experience like a living product. Review it regularly. Gather feedback. Run small experiments. Evolve.

The payoff? When your client experience is designed, predictable, and groomed for empathy, it grows your business's equity, not just its volume.

You aren't just closing deals; you're building something that scales, that creates referrals, that earns retention, and motivates your team. And yes, you're creating something worth selling one day. Client experience may sound like marketing fluff, but in reality, it's one of your most defensible assets.

Free Download: Client Journey Mapping Worksheet

For a free downloadable worksheet to map the entire client journey—from lead to application, pipeline, close, and beyond—go to: dougadlam.com/brokering

Or scan the QR code below:

Chapter 11

Redefining Success—Volume vs. Value

What does it mean to be successful? No, really. Think about it. What does it mean, in your books, to be successful? Does success represent a certain number in your bank account? Is it an award or an accomplishment seen by others? Is it building a business with high revenue? Or is success simply measured by living a comfortable life? Success can mean so many different things, and if you were to ask ten strangers on the street right now what success means to them, you're likely to get ten different answers.

In the world of brokering, success is often measured by the same metric: volume. How many millions did you fund this year? Did you make the top 75 brokers list? Did you win any awards that you can showcase in your reception area or on your website? How many deals did you make and close successfully? Volume can quickly become a bragging right. It's the social media headline and your talking point at industry events. But here's the truth that very few people are willing to admit: Volume without value is just vanity.

I'm not saying this with judgment. I'm guilty of this, too! In my early days as principal broker, I set targets and measured success based on the volume of mortgages. Luckily, the industry is maturing and growing, which means that brokers are redefining what success actually looks like.

They're asking different questions than what we're used to. Instead of focusing solely on volume, they're also focusing on value. They're asking:

- What's your profitability per file?

- What percentage of your business consists of repeat or referral customers?

- Do you have systems that can scale?

- Can your business operate and grow without you?

In this chapter, we'll focus on this shift from volume to value. We'll examine how broker tiers should be tied to more than just numbers, and how broker greed can lead to lender frustration. To make the shift successfully, we also need to analyse why the industry is stuck on volume and how to break the mold and track other things instead. So, buckle up and get ready to make a shift that can change the way you do business forever.

Broker Tiers: More Than Just Numbers

Not every broker is building the same kind of business, and that's a good thing. Some brokers are part-time, managing a few files a year while prioritizing lifestyle and flexibility. Others are solo high-performers, operating lean and efficient businesses with deep client relationships and strong margins. Then you have team leads overseeing small but powerful pods, and brokerage owners building sellable operations with dozens of brokers and staff. Each model requires different strategies, support systems, and mindsets. But here's a critical truth: Comparing volume alone is misleading.

A solo broker funding $30 million in volume annually with 75% of that business coming from repeat and referral clients, minimal burnout, and a healthy 70% profit margin may actually have a far more valuable and sustainable business than a $150 million team that's barely breaking even, experiencing high staff turnover, and bleeding leads from poor client experience. The industry often celebrates top-line volume, but that's only one measure, and often, it's a deceptive one. True business health comes from a combination of profitability, sustainability, client loyalty, and operational efficiency. Without those pillars, high volume can become a trap rather than a triumph.

The key is to define what success looks like for you, not for your mentor, not for your competitor, and not for the award rankings. Your version of success might include more time with your family, less stress, deeper client relationships, or building a business that runs without you. Once you define that target, you can align your operations, pricing model, team structure, and technology to support it. To redefine success for yourself, you need to realize that it's not just about more deals. Instead, it's about securing better deals, implementing better systems, and achieving better alignment with the life and business you want to build.

Broker Greed and Lender Frustration

I recently explored a growing and uncomfortable tension in the mortgage industry: the widening gap between broker behavior and lender expectations. At the heart of this tension lies a misalignment; one that's driven by short-term thinking, ego-driven metrics, and, in some cases, unchecked greed. Some brokers are so focused on chasing volume and awards that they begin cutting corners. Files are rushed, documentation is incomplete, deals are "double-fired" (sent to multiple lenders simultaneously without transparency), and numbers are padded to climb the rankings. It may seem like hustle, but in reality, it's chaos disguised as success.

This kind of behavior not only hurts a broker's relationship with lenders but also undermines the credibility of the entire broker channel. Lenders lose trust, internal teams get bogged down cleaning up messy submissions, and risk managers raise red flags. Eventually, lenders start tightening guidelines or reducing broker access altogether. The painful irony is that brokers who operate this way may see short-term wins, but they're building a house of cards. No lender wants to deepen relationships with brokers who bring friction, unpredictability, or inflated promises. Over time, access dries up, rates become less competitive, and reputations erode.

Lenders are crystal clear about what they want: quality submissions, consistency, transparency, and professionalism. They're not just underwriting files; they're building partnerships. They want brokers who run their businesses with structure and integrity, who respect guidelines, and who care about the borrower's long-term outcome as much as they care about the commission. The brokers who will thrive in the next evolution of this industry aren't the ones with the flashiest numbers. They're the ones building real businesses, ones rooted in efficiency, quality, and aligned incentives.

To be clear, lenders aren't off the hook here. They've contributed to this shift in industry behaviour as well. There was a time when a rate sheet was a rate sheet—firm and final. But as competition between the broker channel and the bank branch channel has intensified, things have changed. Increasingly, the actual rate isn't confirmed until the approval comes back. This allows lenders a second shot at winning the deal, but it also introduces unnecessary inefficiency into the system. In essence, it rewards reactive pricing and undermines loyalty.

Layer on the internal friction within some lenders, particularly between their broker teams and direct-to-consumer divisions, like branches or internal sales forces, and you get even more fragmentation. These internal silos aren't just frustrating; they're contributing to declining efficiency across the board. In a high-cost environment, where both the cost of living and the cost of doing business continue to climb, that's a problem. These practices may drive short-term volume, but they do so at the expense of long-term sustainability. It's a volume-first, margin-later approach, which is a band-aid, not a strategy.

Then there's the client side. As discussed earlier in this book, when there's no clear agreement of understanding between the broker and the client (when expectations around loyalty and commitment haven't been set), it leads to a flood of duplicate submissions. It's now common for the same file to be submitted to the same lender by multiple brokers, or through multiple channels. Add repeated submissions to mortgage default insurers like CMHC, Sagen, and Canada Guaranty, and the situation escalates into chaos. This creates inefficiencies, false red flags for fraud, approval delays, consumer frustration, and yes, upward pressure on mortgage rates.

Regulators, in their efforts to protect consumers, often advocate for maximum rate transparency and shopping flexibility. I don't believe this comes from a bad place. They're trying to ensure fairness and affordability, but what's missing is a macroeconomic view. In reality, this well-intentioned consumer protection model is also contributing to higher costs and interest rates across the board. What's often overlooked is how far this industry has come in terms of professionalism, compliance, and service delivery. The actions of all players (brokers, lenders, insurers, and regulators) shape the overall efficiency and profitability of the ecosystem. Right now, we're all feeling the drag of a system designed for volume, not value.

This industry doesn't need more volume. It needs better value, and that starts with every broker, lender, network, and regulator choosing to lead with integrity.

Why the Industry is Stuck on Volume

I find myself returning to this question again and again: Why is so much of the mortgage industry still fixated on volume as the pinnacle of success? Ask any seasoned business owner, and they'll tell you that volume doesn't pay the bills—revenue does. It's profit that keeps the lights on. A business built purely on volume with thin or negative margins isn't a business built to last. So why the obsession with volume?

First, it's simple to measure. Lenders track funded volume religiously because it's tied to their own internal sales targets. Bonus programs are typically structured around volume tiers, where higher volume equals more basis points, resulting in a higher commission. Scorecards from lenders are volume-based. Marketing awards? Volume-based. Even media and public recognition in the broker world, from "Top 75" lists to brokerage awards, are almost entirely driven by funded dollar amounts. In other words, the entire ecosystem is calibrated to reward volume, even if it's not the best indicator of sustainable success.

To be fair, some lenders do include efficiency metrics in their scorecards, such as approval-to-funding ratios or other submission quality metrics. But these tend to be secondary. The lion's share of broker compensation still hinges on one thing: how many dollars were funded. When incentives are structured that way, it's no surprise that volume becomes the go-to benchmark, even if it doesn't reflect the health, profitability, or scalability of a business. But here's the reality check: Just because something is the default, doesn't mean it's ideal.

It's time for a broader conversation in our industry, one that prioritizes value over volume, client outcomes over leaderboard rankings, and business fundamentals over vanity metrics. Perhaps now that you're in a place of building a business, you can be at the forefront of such important change, pioneering a new era of value over volume.

What Should You Really Be Tracking?

So, if you shouldn't measure everything on volume, what should you be tracking? In any business, including mortgages, the most important metric shouldn't be how much you fund, but how much you keep. Profit is what allows a business to thrive, grow, and scale, and yet, most brokers only glance at profitability annually, if at all. The highest-performing operations take a far more intentional approach. They track profit on a monthly, weekly, and even deal-level basis. They know exactly what every transaction costs and where the dollars are going. This isn't about becoming a spreadsheet junkie, but rather about building clarity and control.

To reach that level of insight, you need better data, and that starts with your CRM. Start by creating custom fields or workflows that capture variable deal costs: legal reimbursements, appraisal fees, inspection costs, cashback incentives, rate buy-downs, and even client gifts. These costs are often absorbed quietly by brokers, especially high producers, and when they're not tracked, they silently chip away at your margins.

The problem is that many brokerage owners don't actually know what each deal is costing them. Even more alarming, they often don't know which team members are profitable and which aren't, given the most typical independent contractor arrangement. That's not just inefficient; it's dangerous. Over the years, I've worked with brokers and owners who made the shift from chasing volume to engineering profitability. One of the most powerful moves they made was leveraging platforms like QuickBooks Online or Xero to track income and expenses in real-time. Then, they use the data and sync it with CRM insights to get a full financial picture. When you pair deal data with financial tracking, you can answer critical questions like:

- Who on the team is consistently buying down rates, and what's the impact on margin?

- Are certain referral sources leading to more costly deals or even no deals at all?

- How much are we spending on reimbursements like appraisals or legal fees, and is that spending strategic?

- Where are we leaking revenue, and what can we do to plug the holes?

- Are team members operating under the same value proposition, or is the brand being diluted by inconsistency?

The answers lie in the numbers. While the truth might be uncomfortable at times, data is your friend. It can help you make better decisions, remove emotion from personnel evaluations, and build a more durable, valuable business. Ultimately, success isn't about volume for volume's sake. It's about running a business that is efficient, profitable, and aligned with your long-term vision.

Advanced Metrics That Matter

If you want to build a truly valuable business, not just a high-volume one, you need to dig deeper into the numbers. Surface-level metrics, such as funded volume or gross commission, are useful, but they don't tell the full story. Value lives in the margins, and the only way to uncover it is through smarter, more precise tracking. Start by focusing on the metrics that reveal real business health, including:

- **Profitability per broker:** This helps you understand who is contributing true value—not just generating revenue, but generating margin. This insight informs your compensation models, coaching priorities, and growth decisions.

- **Average BPS per deal after expenses:** Track this across the entire team, but also drill down by individual broker and by lead source. It will show you which types of deals are actually profitable and where your biggest returns are coming from.

- **Profitability by referral partner:** If you're investing in a referral relationship, whether it's through gifts, meals, event sponsorships, or other gestures (such as your time), you should know if that investment is producing a return. Not all referral sources are created equal, and some may be quietly costing more than they're worth.

- **Cost per lead and cost per funded deal:** Especially if you're using paid lead sources (like Google Ads, Meta campaigns, or purchased leads), it's essential to measure not just how many leads you're getting, but how many convert, and what each funded deal costs you to acquire.

This level of insight is what separates salespeople from business owners. Salespeople chase commissions, but business owners chase margin, sustainability, and scale. That's exactly where long-term business value begins to take shape. When you can see profitability clearly (per deal, per team member, per referral partner), you stop operating on gut feeling and you start building with intention. This will enable you to make sharper hiring decisions, eliminate unproductive partnerships, and double down on what actually works.

Value as a Business Principle

When you shift your mindset from chasing volume to creating value, everything changes; not just your strategy, but your entire approach to building a business. Firstly, you'll start to prioritize long-term client relationships over transactional wins. Instead of aiming to close the deal quickly, you build trust, educate your clients, and become their go-to advisor for years to come—not just their next mortgage, but every financial decision along the way.

Secondly, you'll begin to invest in client experience and brand equity. You stop looking at client touchpoints as checkboxes and start treating them as opportunities to differentiate yourself. A seamless, thoughtful client journey becomes part of your competitive advantage, and your brand becomes something people remember and recommend. Thirdly, you'll track your margins and profitability per deal and stop celebrating annual gross volume. You know which deals, lead sources, and relationships generate the most profit, and which are draining resources.

Lastly, you'll begin to systematize your processes. When you shift your mindset, you begin to understand that scalability isn't about doing more; it's about doing better. You build a repeatable workflow that delivers consistency so your team can operate efficiently and your clients receive the same high standard of service every time. Volume may still come—in fact, it often does—but it's no longer the goal. It becomes the result of doing the right things, the right way, with discipline and clarity.

When you design your business around value, you're not just building a job or chasing rankings. You're building an asset. One that generates profit even when you're not in the room. One that earns loyalty, creates opportunity, and grows in worth over time. One that's resilient, respected, and potentially sellable. This is what separates brokers who hustle endlessly from those who build something truly sustainable. Success isn't just about volume. It's about building with intention and letting value lead the way.

Free Download: Key Metrics Dashboard Template

For a free downloadable Google Sheet with starter metrics and KPIs to track what really matters in your business, go to: dougadlam.com/brokering

Or scan the QR code below:

Chapter 12

Aggregation and Alignment

Aggregation has become one of the most powerful forces in the Canadian mortgage industry over the past decade. What began as a strategic approach to centralize compliance, services, and payroll has now evolved into a defining trait of many modern broker businesses. But aggregation alone isn't enough. It must be paired with alignment. Specifically, alignment in three areas:

- **Alignment of vision**, so that everyone in the organization is moving in the same direction

- **Alignment of values**, so that decisions are made from a shared foundation of belief and purpose

- **Alignment of goals**, so that the growth of the individual contributes meaningfully to the growth of the collective

Without alignment, aggregation can quickly become a liability. It can lead to bloated structures, fractured cultures, and mismatched expectations. Brokers are often drawn into organizations that don't align with their business approach. Teams grow for the sake of growth, not because the pieces truly fit, and in the process, what was meant to create scale and efficiency ends up causing confusion and churn.

This chapter examines why alignment is the true differentiator and how to recognize, cultivate, and safeguard it. We'll unpack the difference between aggregation and integration, examine how to evaluate potential alignment partners, and explore why brokers moving between teams is often a symptom of misalignment, not ambition. Whether you're building a team, joining a network, or stepping into a leadership role within a larger group, alignment isn't a nice-to-have; it's the backbone of a healthy, high-performing business strategy. Let's take a closer look!

Defining Aggregation in the Mortgage Industry

At its core, aggregation refers to the consolidation of multiple brokers or brokerages under a shared umbrella—often a larger brand, national network, or corporate infrastructure. It's a strategy designed to unlock scale by pooling resources, unifying systems, and centralizing support.

Aggregation can take many forms. You can join a regional or national brokerage brand, align with a mortgage network or superbroker platform, partner with a team or sub-brokerage, or partner with a head office to share services like compliance, payroll, technology, marketing, and training.

When done well, aggregation offers powerful advantages, including:

- Stronger lender relationships backed by collective volume

- Enhanced compensation structures through volume-based incentives

- Operational efficiencies via shared compliance systems, admin support, and technology stacks

- Access to innovation through centralized platforms and in-house support teams

- Reduced overhead, allowing brokers and teams to focus more on production and client experience

However, these benefits don't come without very real, very big risks. Some of the risks are:

- Reputational risk with clients, especially when sharing a brand with teams who may operate very differently

- Risk with lenders, particularly when files are submitted under a shared brokerage license or submission agent (one bad apple can affect everyone's relationship)

- Loss of control, as decisions made at the network, brokerage, sub-brokerage, or team level can trickle down to impact your day-to-day operations

In short, aggregation allows you to plug into scale without having to build every piece yourself, but it's not a magic bullet. It introduces new dependencies and potential constraints that can either accelerate your business or slow it down. That's why the conversation can't stop at aggregation. It must go deeper into alignment. Ultimately, the alignment with your possible partner and how well your business vision aligns with theirs determines whether aggregation becomes a strategic advantage or a constant source of friction.

Alignment: The Real Differentiator

In today's mortgage landscape, where aggregation is common, alignment is what sets high-performing brokers apart. Simply joining a larger platform doesn't guarantee success, but joining one that shares your values, vision, and operating philosophy? That's where the magic happens! The brokers and teams who thrive in an aggregated model aren't just benefiting from shared infrastructure; they're doing so without compromising their independence, integrity, or client experience. They've found a partner that amplifies what they already do well, rather than forcing them to adapt to an approach that doesn't fit their business model. Here are key areas you can look for to discover whether you're truly aligned with other parties:

- **Communication style:** Are expectations clearly set and consistently reinforced?

- **Cultural values:** Do you share the same beliefs about how clients should be treated, how business should be done, and what long-term success looks like?

- **Level of autonomy:** Are you empowered to run your business your way, or micromanaged into conformity?

- **Operational expectations:** Do the systems, timelines, and workflows match how you and your team operate?

- **Transparency:** Are compensation, support levels, and performance metrics communicated openly and fairly?

When alignment is strong, everything feels smoother, collaboration improves, trust deepens, and momentum builds. But when it's missing, friction creeps in. Minor irritations compound, and disagreements over process, brand presentation, or compensation evolve into major roadblocks. When this happens, the benefits of aggregation (scale, support, and leverage) are overshadowed by operational stress. So, what's the lesson? Don't just look at what a network or brokerage offers. Look at how well it fits. Alignment isn't a bonus; it's the differentiator that determines whether aggregation accelerates your growth or quietly erodes your business from within.

Choosing the Right Alignment Partner

Throughout my career, I've seen aggregation from every angle: As a solo broker, figuring things out on my own; as a team lead, building systems and scale; as a principal broker, growing a brokerage by 40X; as part of a network-affiliated brokerage; and later, as an executive at a national brand, helping scale from $800M to nearly $4B in volume. Across all those stages, one truth has remained: You have to do your homework.

It's tempting to get swept up by signing bonuses, sleek presentations, or big promises such as "We offer full autonomy," "We have the best tech," or "We'll help you grow faster." But in reality, those surface-level incentives matter far less than two critical factors: cultural and operational fit. The truth is that misalignment costs more than you think. It can drain your energy, slow your growth, and make you second-guess your direction. The right alignment partner should amplify your business, not just attach their logo to it. But how do you know whether someone is the right partner or not? Here's my advice on how to properly vet a potential alignment partner:

- **Don't just talk to the execs:** Ask to speak confidentially with both top producers and mid-tier brokers. You'll get a more honest, balanced view of what it's like inside the organization.

- **Ask about day-to-day support:** Who handles compliance? How quickly do they respond? What happens when a file goes sideways?

- **Dig into operations:** What are the average turnaround times for key processes? How consistent is underwriting if underwriting support is offered? How are internal conflicts managed?

- **Push for transparency:** Are there "special deals" made quietly with certain agents or teams? Are there different rules depending on your production volume or who you know?

- **Explore culture through experience:** What do their team-building events or Professional Development retreats feel like? Is the energy aligned with your own leadership style and vision?

The right partner won't flinch at these questions. In fact, the more transparent and confident they are in answering them, the more likely they are to be a fit for the long haul. This isn't just about finding a better deal. It's about finding a structure that gives your business room to grow with integrity, support, and alignment built in.

Aggregation Isn't Always Integration

It's important to recognize that aggregation and integration are not the same thing. You can join a national brokerage brand and still run a completely independent operation behind the scenes, managing your own back office, choosing your own tech stack, and building your own client journey. In this case, you're aggregated by name, but not by infrastructure. On the flip side, some brokers fully embed themselves within the parent organization, adopting its systems, processes, branding, and support structures. They benefit from centralized efficiency and shared resources, but give up a degree of autonomy in exchange.

Both models can work. Both can create enterprise value. But the key, as always, is alignment—alignment with your business goals, your working style, and your growth strategy. If you crave control and independence, own that. Don't pretend you're looking for deep integration if what you really want is autonomy. You'll only create friction. If you're looking for support and scalability, lean into it. Don't waste time rebuilding systems or resisting structure if the resources already exist. Plug in and maximize them.

Misunderstood expectations, either by the broker or the organization, are where most breakdowns happen. Aggregation can be powerful, but only when your experience aligns with what was promised and what you truly need. The real question isn't "Should I integrate?" It's "What kind of business do I want to build, and does this model support that vision?"

When Brokers Move Between Teams

Within large brokerages or national networks, a unique form of tension can surface when brokers move between teams under the same brand umbrella. While this may seem like a minor internal shuffle, in practice, it can be surprisingly disruptive, both to team culture and to the brand's overall cohesion. So, why does it happen?

In most cases, it comes down to a broker's search for greater alignment, not with the brokerage brand itself, but with the business equity of a particular team. One team might offer stronger systems and operational support. Another might have a culture of collaboration and coaching. Some teams are highly transactional, while others are relationship-driven. The difference between them is often felt more than articulated, but that feeling drives movement.

In my own career, I've seen this dynamic play out in real time. Brokers would ask to transfer teams due to misaligned values or expectations, which creates friction and conflict between team leads when recruitment overlaps or handoffs aren't clearly defined. This, in turn, can lead to talent leaving the brokerage entirely, not because of the brand, but because of misalignment at the team level. These shifts often reveal deeper structural issues, including:

- Vague or inconsistent onboarding processes
- A lack of role clarity across the organization
- No standard for support, communication, or culture across teams

The lesson? Alignment isn't just a top-down concept between broker and brokerage. It needs to exist horizontally, between brokers and the teams they join. Otherwise, the strength of the brand gets diluted by internal disconnection. Smart brokerages and team leads get ahead of this by defining, documenting, and living what their team stands for, how it operates, and what success looks like. That clarity becomes a filter, attracting the right brokers and discouraging the wrong fits before conflict arises.

Alignment as a Business Strategy

Aggregation can unlock tremendous power, yielding more profit, greater influence, and increased prestige, but as we now know, aggregation alone doesn't build lasting value. Alignment does. Whether you're evaluating a national network, exploring a strategic partnership, or building a team within an existing brokerage, the principle remains the same: You can't scale what isn't aligned.

Without alignment, growth creates friction, miscommunication compounds, and operational cracks widen. What could have been an asset becomes a liability—fast. But when alignment is intentional, it becomes a force multiplier. Teams collaborate instead of compete, systems complement instead of clash, and leadership is empowered to focus on strategy rather than constantly putting out fires.

The brokers who go on to build businesses with true enterprise value—the kind that generate profit without their daily involvement and can one day be acquired—are the ones who treat alignment not just as a cultural principle, but as a business strategy.

They choose partners who share their values and operational vision; they create environments where team members know what's expected; they build systems that scale not just in size, but in quality and consistency; and they prioritize profitability and brand integrity over ego and short-term volume. In the end, value is built through unity and not just size. The future of the mortgage industry isn't just about who can aggregate the fastest. It's about who can align the deepest and build something that lasts.

Free Download: Culture Values Worksheet

For a free downloadable worksheet to define your top five company values and begin aligning your business around them, go to: dougadlam.com/brokering

Or scan the QR code below:

Chapter 13

Transparency—The Missing Link in Industry Trust

Transparency has become a bit of a buzzword in the Canadian mortgage industry. It's a word we hear often and that seems to be branded as a value for most. Yet, it's something most people experience very inconsistently. No one seems to argue its importance. If you ask most people, they'll probably say something very appropriate like, "Transparency matters." But the problem comes in that people can't seem to agree on what it actually means to be transparent within your business. If you were to stop and ask ten brokers right now what transparency means, you'd get ten different answers.

The truth is, when we look at the system, it's clear that opacity is baked into it deeply. From compensation structures to value delivery and strategic direction, everything seems to be lacking transparency while claiming to be transparent. But why is that the case? In this chapter, let's aim to put an end to opacity by looking at what transparency means. If you value transparency, it's vital to understand what it means and what it looks like in a business context. This chapter will examine the various types of transparency that are crucial in establishing trust, alignment, and enterprise value. Let's take a closer look in an attempt to become more transparent, shall we?

The Three Types of Transparency

In a high-trust business like mortgage brokering, transparency can't just be a buzzword. It needs to be a foundational pillar of sustainable growth and broker retention. When transparency breaks down, trust erodes, and when trust erodes, performance and loyalty often go with it. Over the years, working with brokers, team leads, and executives across the industry, I've come to recognize three key types of transparency that consistently influence broker confidence and long-term alignment.

Compensation Transparency

Let's start with the most emotionally charged topic: money. What does the brokerage or network actually earn? What does your leadership team get paid? Are you benefiting fairly from the business you bring in? And perhaps most importantly, are there tiers, incentives, or back-end bonuses that not everyone is aware of? These are difficult questions to ask, and even harder to answer honestly. Most brokerages operate with layered and complex compensation structures, making it hard to understand and explain.

There may be multiple tiers that unlock access to higher splits or volume bonuses. Some brokerages may receive overrides or performance-based incentives from lenders that are not widely disclosed. There may be financial kickbacks or revenue-sharing arrangements tied to the use of in-house tools, preferred tech platforms, or certain lenders, all of which are contractually protected under NDAs. And in some cases, access to this information is conditional on status, tenure, or production thresholds. If you haven't "made it" to that level, you simply won't see the whole picture.

Now, let me be absolutely clear: None of this is illegal or unethical by default. In fact, these kinds of tiered arrangements are also common in other industries that reward scale. But the absence of transparency, especially when combined with secrecy, creates a vacuum, and in that vacuum, suspicion breeds. When brokers feel shut out of the financial structure they operate within, they begin to imagine the worst: that others are benefiting unfairly from their efforts, or that their contributions are being undervalued or exploited. This leads to resentment, which can eventually lead to churn.

However, not everyone is entitled to everything, which makes these structures important. Structures are built based on contribution, capital, leadership, and risk, and business owners have the right to design a compensation structure that rewards those elements. The real problem isn't that different people earn different things; it's that no one talks about how or why. So, what's the solution?

No, you don't have to disclose every decimal of your profit margin, but you do need a framework of trust. You need to communicate your philosophy around compensation, including why it's designed the way it is, what brokers can expect at different stages, and how transparency will be handled. When brokers understand the rules of the game, they're far more likely to play it well and stay in it longer. But when they are confused and feel left in the dark, they are more likely to seek transparency elsewhere.

Value Transparency

The second type of transparency is all about delivery. What are you actually offering brokers, and are you delivering what you claim to be? Most companies think they're providing value. In fact, many genuinely believe their value proposition is exceptional. But that belief doesn't matter if the broker's experience says otherwise. Value transparency breaks down when there's a gap between promise and reality. For example:

- When onboarding materials promise robust mentorship, but senior brokers are too busy to answer questions

- When the website shows sleek, modern tech, but in practice, the platform is clunky or unsupported

- When the culture is described as "collaborative," but brokers are left to figure things out on their own

- When support staff are stretched so thin that brokers feel like just another number

- When new brokers flounder while veterans coast, and there's no infrastructure to bridge the gap

All of these examples lead to inconsistency, and inconsistency kills trust.

In most cases, a broker doesn't need perfection, but they do need predictability. If you promise one level of experience and deliver another, the result is disappointment, no matter how good your intentions may be. So, how do you fix it? Start by auditing your broker experience. Don't rely on assumptions or top-down feedback. Have real, open conversations with brokers at every stage of the journey, from new recruits to top producers. Ask them where the gaps are and then be willing to adjust, clarify, or even retract promises that no longer align with reality.

Value transparency means owning your operational truth. When you align your messaging with what you actually deliver, trust becomes much easier to sustain.

Vision Transparency

The third, and often most overlooked, type of transparency is vision. Does your brokerage or network have a clear vision? Do your brokers know what it is? More importantly, does that vision still align with theirs? Vision transparency is about direction, philosophy, and purpose. It answers the deeper questions, such as:

- What are we trying to build here?

- Who do we want to serve?

- What matters most in how we operate?

- Where are we headed over the next three to five years?

The challenge lies in the fact that many brokerages start with one vision and then evolve without communicating the shift. Growth, mergers, leadership transitions, and market forces can all shift the direction of a business, and if brokers aren't kept in the loop, they often feel blindsided by new priorities, new rules, or new cultural expectations.

Misalignment in vision can also lead to subtle disengagement. Brokers don't necessarily leave right away, but they stop participating, stop promoting, and stop investing their energy into the broader brand. They may still produce, but the emotional connection is no longer there.

That's why vision transparency matters. It allows brokers to make informed decisions. It gives them a chance to opt in (or out) before resentment builds. To lead with vision transparency, you don't need to have all the answers. You simply need clarity and consistency in your communication. Let your team know when the path changes. Invite feedback. Create space for healthy dialogue. When brokers feel aligned with the mission, they contribute more fully to it. And when they don't, they can move on with respect and appreciation, rather than confusion or bitterness.

Together, these three types of transparency form the foundation of trust in a broker-centric business. You don't need to be perfect, but you do need to be intentional. The brokers who stay, who grow, and who elevate your brand over time are the ones who feel informed, empowered, and respected. Transparency isn't just a policy; it's a culture, and it's one of the few things that scales with you, no matter how large your business becomes.

Additional Gaps in Transparency

While compensation, value, and vision are the most talked-about pillars of transparency, they're far from the only areas where gaps emerge. In fact, some of the most impactful breakdowns happen not at the top-line strategic level, but in the day-to-day brokerage culture that brokers experience every single day. Let's talk about the promises that are often made during recruitment or onboarding:

- "We're a collaborative culture."

- "We support each other here."

- "You'll have access to mentorship and leadership."

- "We rise together."

These statements are well-intentioned and sometimes even true, but in many organizations, the reality doesn't match the rhetoric. Collaboration, for example, is frequently promoted as a core cultural value, but it is rarely practiced in meaningful, structured ways. Beyond a few Slack messages, surface-level masterminds, or irregular Zoom calls, there's often little follow-through. Brokers are left working in silos, figuring things out on their own, even while surrounded by teammates technically under the same brand.

Mentorship is another area where transparency falls short. The gap between new and experienced brokers continues to widen, and in many brokerages, there's no formal structure in place to close it. New brokers may be promised support but are left waiting for callbacks, piecing together scripts from webinars, or learning critical systems through trial and error. It's not that experienced brokers or team leaders don't want to help. Most do, but many are simply stretched too thin. They're running their own large books of business, managing client expectations, dealing with compliance, and navigating constant change. Supporting others becomes a "nice-to-have," not a business imperative, and without dedicated time, systems, and incentives in place, mentorship becomes passive at best and nonexistent at worst.

This disconnect creates quiet friction. New brokers begin to feel unseen or unsupported. Experienced brokers start to resent being expected to coach without compensation or recognition. Team leaders, stuck in the middle, carry the emotional weight of wanting to lead but lacking the bandwidth to do so well. Eventually, that friction becomes disillusionment, and disillusionment leads to churn—not because the opportunity wasn't real, but because the delivery didn't match the promise.

This is what unspoken gaps in transparency look like in practice. They're not always dramatic. In fact, they're often subtle, invisible even, but over time, they erode trust and performance just as surely as financial ambiguity or strategic misalignment. If brokers don't know what to expect, whether it be from leadership, from their peers, or from their day-to-day experience, they can't fully commit. And if they don't commit, they won't stay.

Why Transparency Matters More Than Ever

Transparency is no longer a bonus trait of forward-thinking leaders. It's becoming a non-negotiable in the future of mortgage aggregation. As consolidation accelerates and aggregators wield more influence, the cost of misalignment gets steeper. The brokerage landscape is shifting, and brokers are more informed, more skeptical, and more selective than ever before. They don't just want to know what they're getting paid. They want to know why decisions are being made, how values are practiced, and who will truly have their back when the market turns.

In this environment, trust becomes your most valuable business asset, and transparency is the operating system that builds and maintains it. Let's be clear: Transparency doesn't mean spilling every detail of your financial model or handing over your proprietary systems. It doesn't mean radical openness at the expense of strategy. What it does mean is creating shared understanding, clear, consistent expectations, and most importantly, alignment between what you say and what you do.

When a brokerage is transparent about its structure, support systems, expectations, and limitations, it doesn't scare people away, but it attracts the right people. It builds a community where brokers can self-select into the culture that fits them best, rather than getting sold into something that never existed. I strongly believe that the most valuable brokerages in the next decade won't be the ones with the flashiest tech, the highest signing bonuses, or the most aggressive splits. They'll be the ones with the clearest vision, the most consistent delivery, the highest-trust culture, and the biggest budgets to reinvest into creating value for their team members. The brokerages where people know what to expect and what's expected of them. The places where alignment isn't just a pitch; it's a practice.

In an industry this competitive and complex, clarity is your guiding light. Transparency may feel uncomfortable at times. It may require tougher conversations and more nuanced communication. But the payoff is worth it.

Free Download: Improving Transparency Exercise

For a free downloadable exercise to identify where transparency is lacking in your organization, rate the impact, and propose solutions, go to: dougadlam.com/brokering

Or scan the QR code below:

Chapter 14

Lender Partnerships and Sustainable Compensation

Strong lender relationships aren't a luxury in the mortgage brokerage business—they're a necessity. Yet, many brokers approach lenders as if they were simply order-takers, treating each interaction as a one-off transaction. The reality is far more nuanced. Lenders are not just vendors; they are strategic partners in your business growth. This shift in mindset—from viewing lenders as external service providers to seeing them as essential allies—changes everything. It transforms the tone of conversations, the quality of collaboration, and ultimately, the outcomes for clients.

In this chapter, we'll discuss why partnerships are important and why they shouldn't be seen as a once-off transaction. We'll also discuss sponsorships, the cost of revenue distribution, and what a sustainable partnership should look like. Remember, you're building something to scale and eventually sell, which means you have to consider all of these elements to create a business worth selling.

A Pivotal Lesson in Partnership

One of the most formative lessons I received early in my mortgage career came from my parents. They said, "Lenders are partners, not just pipelines. They want to lend money just as much as you want to close deals. Respect that drive, and treat them accordingly."

That lesson only really hit home long after they said it, during a car ride to an industry event. I had the opportunity to ride with a business development manager from one of the big lenders, and over a few hours, I gained rare insight into the daily challenges they face, such as meeting volume goals, navigating corporate politics, handling broker requests, and often juggling more than anyone realizes. That experience made me realize just how much brokers tend to overlook the human side of lending.

When we begin to understand the pressure our lender contacts operate under, we start treating them less like vending machines and more like collaborators. In other words, we start to build human connections and relationships. I never would've gained such insights in my career if I hadn't intentionally spent time with my lender partners and had in-depth, in-person conversations. Emails are fast, and phone calls are efficient, but nothing builds trust quite like sitting across the table from someone. Whether it's a quick coffee, a working lunch, or a broader roundtable meeting, meeting someone face-to-face is invaluable, especially when it comes to your lender partners.

Interactions like these allow for more than updates on rates or policies. They open the door to real dialogue about product development, service pain points, and mutual growth. They also reveal what truly drives your lender partners: their goals, limitations, compensation structures, and internal pressures. Understanding these dynamics helps you become a better partner to them; one who supports, rather than just requests.

The Sponsorship Conversation

Now it's time to tackle a touchy subject: compensation and sponsorship. For many brokerages, these have become hot-button issues, sources of both opportunity and strain. Broker compensation has risen steadily over the last two decades. Volume tiers have climbed, incentive programs have multiplied, and sponsorship expectations are now baked into almost every brokerage-lender relationship. But here's the reality: The well is not bottomless.

Lenders are facing mounting financial pressure. Compressed margins, rising capital costs, increased regulatory requirements, and the need for ongoing tech investment have changed the equation. And yet, the asks keep coming—more money for events, higher compensation, and sometimes, ambiguous returns on those investments. What many brokers don't see is the internal tension this creates. Business development managers are caught in the middle, trying to keep brokers happy while justifying budgets to their leadership. Lenders are being asked to give more without any guarantees that the relationship will deepen, the volume will increase, or the quality of submissions will improve.

This dynamic creates an imbalance. A partnership built solely on financial demands is not a partnership; it's a transaction, and transactional relationships don't survive market shifts. We must ask ourselves: Are we creating partnerships that generate mutual value, or are we draining our lender relationships without reinvesting? Sponsorship dollars and compensation should be seen as tools to enhance strategic alignment, not entitlements. Brokers and broker owners need to articulate the business case for sponsorships: What's the return for the lender? How does the investment improve outcomes for both parties?

A better approach is transparency and collaboration. Don't just ask for money, but outline your vision, your growth strategy, your plan to expand market share or improve client service. Make lenders part of your business roadmap. Equally important, show appreciation. Too often, sponsorships are taken for granted. A simple thank-you, a progress report, or a candid check-in can go a long way in reinforcing trust. The bottom line? Sustainable partnerships require balance, respect, and shared risk. If you're demanding more from your lender, be ready to give more in return—in loyalty, quality, and long-term engagement.

The Cost of Revenue Distribution

In recent years, the brokerage industry has trended toward higher and higher broker splits (90/10, 95/5, and even higher in rare cases) as brokerages compete to attract top producers. On the surface, these splits seem to favor brokers, offering greater financial reward for their individual performance. But beneath that shiny exterior lies a harsh reality: These ultra-high splits are eroding the financial foundation of many brokerages.

Running a professional, compliant, and forward-thinking mortgage operation is not a low-overhead endeavor. There are fixed and variable costs that can't be ignored, such as business insurance, compliance management, fraud prevention, regulatory audits, tech subscriptions, CRM systems, payroll for support staff, training programs, legal and accounting services, professional development, and marketing infrastructure. These are not luxuries; they're essential for delivering a high-quality client experience and meeting industry standards.

Yet in a model where such a high percentage of revenue is funneled directly to the broker, the remaining margin often doesn't cover basic operational costs. What happens then? Corners get cut. Compliance risks rise, training gets neglected, and instead of building a sellable, sustainable business, brokerages become fragile shells, operating on hope and volume. Many brokerage owners know this, but too many are hesitant to take action, afraid to challenge the status quo for fear of losing top earners to competitors. The problem is, by avoiding those tough conversations, they're often trading short-term retention for long-term ruin. To create a thriving business, owners need to lead with clarity and courage. That means:

- Explaining the true cost of operations so brokers understand where the money goes

- Being honest about margin constraints and the impact on tools, service, and support

- Creating tiered compensation structures that reward performance while protecting sustainability

- Being confident enough to defend their right to earn a return on their investment and associated risk

It's not about gutting broker compensation. It's about balance. Brokers should earn well, but not at the expense of brokerage viability. After all, if the brokerage collapses, everyone loses. The most resilient brokerages of the future will be those that don't just chase volume but build a solid financial model that supports growth, compliance, and innovation. Broker splits should be part of a broader conversation—a conversation about partnership, value creation, and building something that lasts.

Sustainable Business Models

As I just said, there's nothing wrong with brokers earning strong compensation. But expecting more from every stakeholder, including lenders, brokerages, and support teams, without increasing your own contribution simply isn't sustainable. It's not about slashing comp, but about creating a business structure that can scale without imploding. To achieve this sustainable model and balance, brokerages must:

- Be clear about how and where revenue is allocated

- Build in a margin for growth and resilience

- Develop reciprocal relationships with lenders

- Define and uphold service standards internally

Furthermore, as an industry, we must all recognize that lenders are not unlimited resources, that strong relationships beat short-term leverage, and that profitability is a team sport. The most future-ready brokerages will be those that get this balance right. You might not get it right immediately, but if you build your business with this in mind, you're setting yourself up for success in the future.

What Sustainable Partnership Looks Like

A truly healthy lender partnership goes far beyond the numbers on a comp sheet or how many files you send their way. It's about creating a relationship rooted in trust, shared goals, and mutual respect. What does that look like in practice? It means both sides show up ready to contribute, not just collect. It's a two-way street: Lenders support your growth, and you help them reach their targets through clean files, thoughtful communication, and proactive collaboration.

It also means understanding the value of strategic alignment. Are your business models complementary? Do your client philosophies match up? When both broker and lender are heading in the same direction, the partnership becomes a multiplier, not a drain. Equally important are boundaries. Strong partners don't manipulate volume or threaten to move business to gain leverage. They respect that the relationship needs to work financially and operationally for both sides. That doesn't mean avoiding hard conversations; it means having them with honesty and goodwill.

The brokers who build exceptional lender relationships are often the quiet achievers. They send in clean, complete files that reduce back-and-forth. They offer feedback that's constructive, not combative, they show up when it matters, not just when bonuses are on the table, and they treat account managers, underwriters, fulfilment officers, and funders like human beings, not tools to be used. In today's market, where product differences are shrinking and competition is fierce, the strength of your relationships can be your ultimate edge. Rates can often be matched. Service can be copied. However, trust—real trust—is earned through consistent and thoughtful partnership. And that's what truly moves the needle.

The Need for a Shift

What we need to make this happen is a cultural shift. We need to shift our focus from chasing every extra basis point to building durable, trusting partnerships. We need to move away from squeezing margins and toward sharing accountability. The best brokers I've seen are already doing this. They give before they ask. They support their lenders during tough quarters. They find creative ways to add value. Most importantly, they understand that building something that lasts means lifting everyone involved.

Focusing only on compensation is very short-term thinking, while focusing on mutually beneficial relationships is long-term strategy. Our industry gets caught in short-term thinking all the time, but we have to be confident in our industry and in our businesses to think long term, plan longer term, and build lasting relationships.

So, let's reframe the questions. It's not just "What can my lender do for me in the short term?" Rather, let's ask, "What can we build together that can endure, scale, and serve our clients better for the long term?" Because real compensation isn't just what you make, it's what you sustain. That's the future of brokering that we should aim to build together.

Free Download: Partnership Self-Assessment Tool

For a free downloadable tool to evaluate whether your partnerships are transactional or sustainable, go to: dougadlam.com/brokering

Or scan the QR code below:

PART THREE
SELL

Chapter 15

What Makes a Mortgage Business Sellable?

What makes a business attractive to a buyer?

This is a question every mortgage broker should be asking, not just at the end of their career, but from the very beginning. The cold, hard truth is that your business is only worth what someone else is willing to pay for it. People don't just want to buy a job; they want to buy a system that produces results with or without you at the helm. We already know that many mortgage professionals build businesses that are entirely dependent on their personal relationships and daily involvement, so we know what doesn't sell. But that then begs the question: What makes a mortgage business sellable?

That's exactly what this chapter is for. We'll look at how to position your business for a future transaction, whether that's a full exit, a merger, or a strategic acquisition. You'll learn who's buying, what they're really looking for, and how to prepare your business now for maximum value later. We'll also tackle the common friction points, like term contracts, dual agreements, and the accounting practices that can either elevate or erode your sale price. Whether you're five years away from exiting or just starting to think like an owner instead of an operator, this chapter is your roadmap to building a mortgage business that's not just successful but sellable.

Institutional Readiness

In the world of business acquisitions, one concept carries significant weight: institutional readiness. This refers to a company's ability to operate, grow, and produce consistent, predictable results without relying on the daily involvement of its founder or key personality. If your mortgage business revolves entirely around your name, your client relationships, and your personal hustle, what you have isn't truly a business; it's a job. And jobs can't be sold. At best, they can be wound down or handed off informally. Serious buyers, especially institutional ones, are looking for systems, not personalities.

Now, it is technically possible to sell a business that's closely tied to the owner's personal brand. But those businesses almost always sell for less (often significantly less) because the buyer is taking on greater risk. If the business disappears the moment the owner walks out the door, there's no real asset being transferred.

The good news is that institutional readiness can be built. With strategic foresight and deliberate changes, such as shifting the brand identity away from the individual, documenting processes, strengthening team leadership, and diversifying referral sources, it's entirely possible to transform a personality-driven operation into a sellable business. The earlier you start this process, the more leverage and value you'll have when the time comes to exit.

Who Buys Mortgage Businesses?

We've been paying a lot of attention to making your business sellable, but to whom? Who will actually be interested in buying a mortgage business? One of the most common misconceptions in our industry is that the only potential buyers for a mortgage business are large broker networks or national franchises. While those players are certainly active in the market, they're far from the only ones. In reality, many buyers are other brokers, often boutique brokerage owners or top-producing agents, who are looking to grow their volume, expand into new markets, or acquire an existing team and infrastructure. These are entrepreneurial individuals who see acquisition as a strategic shortcut to scale, rather than building everything from scratch.

These types of buyers are far more likely to pay a premium for a business that is institutionally ready. In other words, they are looking for businesses that are not overly reliant on the founder, have a transferable brand, documented systems and workflows, and a proven track record of stable, predictable performance. Whether the buyer is a major network or a local competitor looking to grow, they all want the same thing: a business they can step into and run (or integrate) without everything falling apart the moment the original owner steps away.

Why is this important to know? Because understanding who your buyer might be is the first step toward building a business they'll actually want to purchase. You can't cultivate something for a specific target audience if you don't know who the audience is.

Dual Agreements: Structuring for Saleability

In today's mortgage industry, it's common for top-producing brokers to operate a semi-independent business within a larger licensed brokerage. These brokers often run their own teams, build their own brands, and manage their own client pipelines, all while technically working under someone else's brokerage umbrella. This hybrid structure can work well operationally, but it becomes tricky when you're thinking about selling the business. That's where clear, dual-layer agreements become essential. You don't need to own a brokerage license to build a sellable business, but you do need formal structures in place to define how your team operates. Ideally, there should be two distinct agreements:

- **The Brokerage Agreement:** This is the formal contract required by regulation between each individual broker and the licensed brokerage with which they are registered. It covers compliance, licensing, and regulatory responsibilities.

- **The Internal Team Agreement:** This is the contract between the broker and the team leader or business owner with whom they work, the one who actually oversees their day-to-day operations. This agreement outlines the compensation structure, roles and responsibilities, expectations regarding lead generation and branding usage, and, most importantly, ownership of the book of business.

This second agreement is critical for valuation and saleability. It clearly defines who controls the client relationships, revenue streams, and systems that drive business performance. Without it, buyers are left guessing, or worse, assuming that the team could unravel as soon as the original leader exits. Think of these agreements as your business scaffolding. They don't just protect your operations today, but they also create the legal and operational clarity that future buyers demand. If your goal is to sell one day, putting these dual agreements in place now is one of the smartest moves you can make. But remember, if you are a brokerage owner, the details contained in the team agreement roll up into the brokerage agreement.

Term Contracts vs. Open Contracts

The mortgage industry is deeply divided on the question of whether brokers should operate under term contracts or open (non-binding) agreements. Each approach has its merits, but the decision significantly impacts business stability and saleability. Open contracts offer brokers maximum flexibility. They allow individuals to leave at any time if they feel the business is no longer delivering value. This forces brokerage owners and team leaders to stay sharp, continuously earning loyalty through service, support, culture, and opportunity. It's a model that fosters innovation and responsiveness, keeping the business accountable to the broker experience.

However, term contracts come with a different kind of value; one rooted in predictability and long-term planning. For the business owner, term agreements offer greater revenue stability, reduce churn risk, and make it possible to invest more confidently in systems, marketing, training, professional development, and growth initiatives. These contracts aren't about locking people in; they're about aligning interests over a defined period. From the broker's perspective, a term contract provides clarity. It outlines exactly what they're receiving—from compensation to support to lead flow—and sets a timeline to revisit and renegotiate terms. It formalizes expectations and reinforces mutual accountability.

Some people mistakenly assume that revisiting compensation only benefits the sales-producing broker. In truth, it can benefit the business just as much, if not more. When you build a structure where performance is tracked and profitability per broker is reviewed regularly, you create room for thoughtful rewards and the ability to address underperformance constructively. At the end of the day, every player in the mortgage ecosystem, from broker networks to lenders to individual teams, is running a business. Shared success is the only path to a thriving industry, and strong contracts, whether open or term-based, are essential tools to ensure that everyone's expectations are aligned and respected. Let's recap the difference between Open Contracts and Term Contracts.

Aspect	Open Contracts	Term Contracts
Broker Flexibility	High: Brokers can leave at any time	Moderate: Commitment for a set period
Business Stability	Lower: Less predictability, higher churn risk	Higher: More predictable revenue and broker retention
Incentive for Innovation	Strong: Businesses must constantly earn loyalty	Moderate: Innovation tied to long-term investment strategy
Revenue Predictability	Limited: Harder to forecast income	Strong: Enables long-term planning and business investment
Performance Tracking	Informal: Loyalty is often based on relationships	Formal: Structured reviews and renegotiations at contract renewal
Broker Expectations	Often vague or implied	Clearly defined: Roles, support, and compensation are explicitly stated
Valuation Impact	Lower: Seen as higher risk by institutional buyers	Higher: Buyers prefer businesses with formal contracts and lower churn risk
Ideal For	Agile teams, new brokerages, or relationship-based businesses	Sellable, sale-ready firms, or businesses investing in structured growth

What Institutional Buyers Look For

To further help you build a business that can be sold, here's exactly what institutional buyers are looking for and evaluating your business on:

- **Repeatable Processes:** Buyers want to see that the business follows consistent, documented workflows, from lead generation and application intake to deal structuring, submission, and post-close follow-up. Repeatable processes reduce risk, ensure consistency, and make the business easier to scale.

- **Systematized Technology:** A sellable CRM and DMS are essential. Institutional buyers expect clearly defined workflows, automation where appropriate, and good data hygiene. They don't want to inherit a digital mess; they want infrastructure that supports growth.

- **Role Clarity:** Defined roles and responsibilities across the team are critical. Ideally, there are job descriptions, performance expectations, KPIs (key performance indicators), and SOPs (standard operating procedures). This clarity not only supports efficient operations but also ensures continuity when team members transition in or out.

- **Owner Optionality:** A business that can only function with its founder at the center isn't really a business. Buyers want a company that runs independently, with strong team leadership, empowered staff, and reliable relationships with lenders and service providers. The less the business depends on you, the more it's worth.

- **Brand Independence:** Businesses that are branded around a single individual are harder to sell and transfer. Institutional buyers look for brands that are distinct from the founder, with a presence that clients and referral partners trust regardless of who's in charge.

WHAT MAKES A MORTGAGE BUSINESS SELLABLE?

- **Predictable Cash Flow:** One common misconception is that commission-based businesses can't offer predictability. That's not true. Buyers look for consistent monthly deal flow, a track record of stable revenue, documented trailer fee income, and systems that support ongoing performance. Predictability doesn't require guaranteed income; it requires operational discipline and history.

- **Community Integration:** For locally focused mortgage businesses, embedded community relationships are a valuable asset. Involvement in local charities, sponsorships of sports teams, and collaborations with educational institutions aren't just good optics; they create brand equity, expand the referral network, and signal long-term commitment to the market.

The Accountant's Dilemma

Most traditional accounting firms struggle to accurately value mortgage broker businesses. Their default approach of examining two to four years of historical profit and applying a discounted cash flow (DCF) model is common in traditional industries, but it is insufficient in this one. Why? Because accountants often undervalue the less tangible but highly critical elements that drive a mortgage business's future success, such as systems, people, brand strength, and scalability.

Consider this: A manufacturing company has no guaranteed future orders, yet it's still valued based on its operational capability and client base. A mortgage brokerage is no different, yet it is treated differently. The key factor isn't whether the income is commission-based; it's whether the business is built to deliver repeatable, transferable, and sellable value, and that can be quantified. If you want to command a strong sale price, not just a small premium on recent earnings, your business must demonstrate value beyond a spreadsheet. That means building systems that allow for consistent client experience, compliance, and pipeline management. As well as creating a brand that stands on its own, and one that clients and partners trust, even if you're not involved.

Additionally, it also means documenting processes and delegating execution so the business can operate without you at the center, and proving profitability and growth potential, not just based on your hustle, but on your infrastructure and team. The traditional accountant's lens may overlook these factors, but sophisticated buyers won't. They're looking for a business, not a job. Make sure you've built one.

Another reason why accountants might undervalue mortgage businesses occurs during mergers and acquisitions. General accountants and independent business evaluators often misunderstand mortgage business economics. While traditional valuation models work well for retail stores, manufacturing businesses, or subscription-based service companies, it's harder to fit a mortgage brokerage into a neat and tidy box. Commission-based businesses, such as this one, with the majority of revenue paid up front, are often dismissed as unpredictable or unsellable, but the truth is that many mortgage businesses have more stable operations than their valuation suggests.

But then, why do accountants miss it? Because this stability is found in the systems, people, and repeatable performance, and not in the contracts. Accountants struggle with understanding that commission-based cash flow often comes with a lag cycle, meaning that some months the books might look bad, even though it was a good month. Evaluating trailing income can be tricky, and interpreting CRM and deal pipelines can seem impossible. Unfortunately, the result of this is that businesses are undervalued or wrongly dismissed as too volatile to invest in.

That's why it's important to work with professionals who understand the true drivers of value in the mortgage sector. Whether it's an advisor, a strategic partner, or a specialized accountant, make sure your deal team knows how to evaluate.

Everything Is Fixable

Not every mortgage business is sale-ready today, and that's perfectly normal. Institutional readiness is a journey, not a switch you flip overnight. The good news? Every challenge on that path is solvable. If your brand is currently built around your name, you don't have to erase your identity. Rebrand slowly and strategically. Transition to a name and message that reflect the business, not just the person behind it.

If you're still the primary broker and rainmaker, you can start to build a team and leadership structure. Train others to handle client work, manage relationships, and make decisions without your constant involvement. Additionally, if your processes are mostly in your head, begin documenting them right now! Standardize your workflows, build out your systems, and make it easier for others to follow and eventually take over.

The point is that it's doable. Everything is fixable. With time, focused efforts, and the right support, any broker can evolve from being a self-employed producer to a business owner, and from a business owner into someone who can successfully exit if and when they want to. Even if you're not planning on selling tomorrow, building for institutional readiness creates options. It gives you leverage, peace of mind, and value that isn't tied solely to your daily grind. You don't need to have everything perfect; you just need to start moving in the right direction.

Free Download: Business Sale Readiness Checklist

For a free downloadable checklist outlining the key factors that make your business attractive to buyers, go to: dougadlam.com/brokering

Or scan the QR code below:

Chapter 16

The Exit Shift—From Operator to Architect

There's a common misconception in the mortgage industry that "exit" is synonymous with retirement. It's seen as a final step, slowing down, or walking away. But that view is outdated and limiting. In truth, exit isn't about ending at all. It's about evolving. For many high-performing mortgage professionals, exit planning is less about stepping away forever and more about creating freedom. It's about designing a business that doesn't rely on your constant presence. It's about reclaiming your time, leveraging your legacy, and unlocking the ability to shift, whether that means scaling something new, focusing on strategic growth, or simply taking a breath.

The real shift isn't just operational; it's also psychological. It's the transition from operator to architect. From being in the weeds to building the blueprint. This chapter explores what it takes to make that shift: how burnout often forces the conversation, what happens in the first days after real delegation, and why exit planning should be viewed as a strategic lever, not a final goodbye. Ultimately, the power isn't in leaving. The power is in having the option to. So, if you're considering or busy building a business that's sellable, listen up because the most challenging part might just be doing the thing you've planned to do for so long: letting go.

The Burnout-Driven Shift

There's a lot of negative connotation with the word "burnout." It's thrown around carelessly after a rough week or even a rough day. But burnout is more than just being tired, and it affects every aspect of your life. Oh, and it's very real. Burnout doesn't just go away after a good nap or a plate of steamed veggies. It can linger and worsen for months or even years. Unfortunately, burnout is very common in the mortgage industry, where the pace is relentless and the boundaries between work and life blur fast. For brokers who have spent years grinding through evenings, weekends, and nonstop client demands, the passion that once fueled the business can quietly erode under the constant weight of urgency.

As mentioned earlier in this book, I had my own experience with burnout in 2016. While everything looked great on paper, I was emotionally exhausted, physically drained, and beginning to feel like a prisoner of my own success. The business that once felt like a calling had started to feel like a cage. While burnout isn't fun, it did have a silver lining as it forced me toward a turning point. Instead of continuing down a path of compounding stress, I went back to the beginning. I pulled out the original business plan I had written in 2007 and began reimagining what my next chapter could look like. For me, to exit wasn't about quitting. It was about building something sustainable. It was about creating a business that could fuel my creativity, protect my energy, and allow me to lead with purpose again.

What I wish I knew was that I didn't have to wait for burnout, and neither do you. You don't have to wait until there's no other option left before you start considering exiting. You don't need to hit a wall, face a personal crisis, or run out of steam before making a shift. The best time to redesign your business is before you reach the breaking point. Make time now, not later, to reflect on what you truly want from this business. Not just financially, but also emotionally and energetically. The earlier you start, the more freedom you'll have to shape a business that supports your life, not the other way around.

Three Days Post-Delegation

I remember it clearly: Just three days after I fully delegated the operations of our business, I felt like a different person. The fog lifted. The constant mental noise, like checklists, client files, and admin tasks, suddenly quieted. Instead, it was replaced with clarity, creativity, and something I hadn't felt in a long time: joy. The shift was almost immediate despite the looming fear that it would fail. Ideas started flowing again. I could think strategically, not just reactively. I found myself energized by the possibility of what could come next, rather than drained by the demands of the day-to-day. For the first time in years, I didn't feel guilty for taking time to step back, reflect, or simply breathe.

Delegation wasn't just a smart business move; it was transformational. It gave me the space to lead instead of manage. To grow instead of grind. To dream again. And the more time passed after that initial delegation, the more I realized something powerful: My capacity to innovate didn't just return, it multiplied! That's the true power and promise of exit. It's not absence, but optionality. It's not about stepping away from your business forever, but about stepping into the freedom to choose how you want to engage, where you can add value, and what exactly you want to build next.

By stepping back and delegating, I felt more like myself within three days than I had in years. I'm not saying it will be exactly the same way for you, as we're all different. What I am saying is that it doesn't have to feel like "giving up" or being bored. It can actually feel like a brand-new beginning, filled with opportunities and excitement.

Exit as a Strategic Lever

There's a tendency in this industry to think of "exit" as a final chapter—a finish line that signals the end of your professional journey. But that's a narrow view. In reality, exit is a strategic lever. One you can use to gain control over your time, energy, and future direction. For high-performing mortgage professionals, exit isn't about stepping away from the game. It's about choosing how, when, and where to play next. For some, exit does mean a complete sale and a clean break. For others, it's a gradual retreat, like shifting into a strategic advisory role or maintaining equity without daily involvement. It could also mean removing yourself from operations to focus on higher-leverage opportunities: public speaking, coaching, consulting, real estate investing, or even launching an entirely different venture. The point isn't to retire. The point is to reclaim your freedom on your terms.

In my own journey, the power of this lever became clear through experience. When we launched our fintech company, we did so with a 36-month exit plan in mind. That goal influenced everything, including the structure, the team, the technology, and even our marketing strategy. We built the business for transferability from day one. Just past the three-and-a-half-year mark, we sold it. That wasn't luck. It was the result of building with intentionality and keeping the end in mind the entire way through.

My mortgage business followed a similar philosophy, although the timeline was less defined. I wasn't in a rush to sell, but I knew I wanted the option. So I designed the business with that flexibility built in: I ensured it was branded for transferability, supported by strong team members, and equipped with documented CRM-supported processes that didn't depend on me. That approach allowed me to step back gradually, test new roles, and eventually walk away without jeopardizing what we'd built. Even in my foray into wealth management, where I initially expected to stay long-term, the exit lever came into play. As my passion shifted, I realized I no longer wanted to lead that business. More importantly, I saw that my continued presence was starting to limit the growth of others. That realization was humbling, but it was also freeing. By stepping aside, I created space for new leadership to emerge and for myself to pursue new opportunities with clarity and energy.

What I've learned through these transitions is this: Exit is a mindset, not a moment. You don't need a buyer lined up to start planning. You don't even need to be certain about when you'll leave. You just need to build your business so that you can, if and when you choose to. That's what gives you true freedom: the power to decide. So, whether your ideal timeline is three years, ten years, or unknown, the time to start thinking about exit is now, because the sooner you design for it, the more options you'll have. Exit isn't an ending. It's a tool for transformation; one that lets you evolve, expand, and engage with your next chapter from a place of strength.

From Founder to Builder

The most successful exits don't come from people who simply run businesses—they come from those who build them. There's a fundamental difference between being the founder of a company and becoming its architect. Founders often start by doing everything: originating deals, managing relationships, and solving daily fires. Builders step back and design a structure that can run without them. They create something sellable, repeatable, and transferable. This shift requires more than just better systems. It demands a change in mindset, priorities, and the metrics you use to define success. It means shifting your focus from personal production to business performance.

Instead of asking, "How much did I close this month?" Start asking questions like:

- How much did the business close this month?

- How consistently are we executing our systems?

- How confident am I in my team's ability to operate independently?

- What are our clients saying, not about me, but about the brand and service experience as a whole?

These questions reflect a maturing leadership perspective. One that recognizes the value in relinquishing control to build something that endures beyond the founder. But it's not easy. Many high-performing brokers struggle with the idea of not being at the center of every transaction. However, real freedom doesn't come from being indispensable. It comes from building something that thrives without your constant involvement. Exit readiness isn't just operational; it's also emotional. It requires the maturity to trust others, the clarity to define your next chapter, and the courage to release your grip on what you've built. When you move from founder to builder, you unlock the potential not only for sale but for sustainable impact and true entrepreneurial freedom.

The Option Is the Win

What exactly is this chapter trying to tell you? Well, it's this: You don't have to sell your business. You don't have to walk away. You don't need to set a retirement date or announce your next chapter. But you do need the option.

That's the true power of an exit-ready business: choice. It puts you back in the driver's seat, giving you the ability to pivot, pause, or pass the torch on your own terms. Whether you ultimately decide to stay involved, scale up, scale down, or cash out, the fact that you have the option makes all the difference. Exit readiness isn't just about preparing for the end. It's about unlocking freedom in the present. It's about knowing that if a life-changing opportunity arrives, whether personal or professional, you're not stuck. You're not tethered to the day-to-day. You've built something that can stand without you. And that's the win.

So, don't wait for the perfect moment. Don't wait until burnout forces your hand. Start now. Design a business with freedom embedded into its foundation, build systems that run without you, and empower people who grow beyond you. Shape a brand that lives without your constant presence so that when the time does come, and it will, you'll be ready. And that confidence, that flexibility, that option? That's the real success.

Free Download: Freedom to Re-Allocate Your Time Exercise

For a free downloadable exercise to explore how you would re-allocate your time—across business, family, friends, and community—once you've stepped out of day-to-day sales, go to: dougadlam.com/brokering

Or scan the QR code below:

Chapter 17

Mergers, Acquisitions, and Partnerships

Mergers and acquisitions aren't just for banks and tech giants. They're becoming increasingly common in the mortgage brokering industry as well. Whether you're considering a full acquisition, exploring a strategic merger, or forming a revenue-sharing partnership, the landscape is evolving and the stakes are high. When executed well, these deals can accelerate growth, expand market reach, and create long-term value for all parties involved. Done poorly, they can lead to misalignment, reputational risk, and the slow unraveling of what was once a high-performing business.

This chapter is designed to demystify the world of mergers and acquisitions (M&A) and strategic partnerships. We'll define the key terms, break down the difference between acquiring and being acquired, explore how to assess alignment before joining forces, and walk through the foundational elements of a well-structured deal. You'll also learn the critical role leadership plays in post-deal integration and the red flags to watch for before you sign anything. Whether you're preparing to scale through acquisition, looking to exit through sale, or simply exploring your options, understanding how these deals work (and how to structure them in your favor) is essential. So, let's take a closer look and make sure we're fully familiar with mergers, acquisitions, and partnerships.

What Do They Really Mean?

Before exploring strategy and structure, it's essential to clarify three terms that are often used interchangeably but carry distinct implications: merger, acquisition, and partnership.

- **Merger:** A merger occurs when two or more businesses come together to form a new, unified entity. In most cases, this involves blending leadership teams, operations, and resources, often under a new or co-branded identity. Mergers are typically pursued when each business brings a similar size (but not necessarily), market presence, or complementary strengths to the table. The goal is mutual growth, synergy, and shared equity.

- **Acquisition:** An acquisition is when one business purchases all of or controlling interest in another. This can take the form of a full buyout, a majority stake acquisition, or even a minority stake position. Unlike a merger, acquisitions tend to retain one business's leadership and brand while folding the acquired company into existing systems and structures. The acquiring company usually sets the terms, vision, and direction post-sale.

- **Partnership:** A partnership involves a formal agreement between two or more businesses to work together without exchanging equity or merging operations. This might look like a shared marketing campaign, co-branded events, joint referral systems, shared services, or even pooled mortgage volumes. Each business maintains its independence, but agrees to collaborate in clearly defined ways to drive mutual benefit.

Understanding these distinctions matters. Whether you're entering negotiations or just starting to explore options, clarity on what each model entails helps ensure you align your goals and protect your business from the start.

Acquire vs. Acquired: Two Perspectives

There is a big difference between acquire and acquired. While they might sound similar, they are two very different experiences and perspectives. In your life, you might find yourself on either side of the coin, but it's vital to have an understanding of what the other party is experiencing, not just what you are perceiving.

The acquirer is typically focused on growth, stability, and scalability. Their lens is strategic as they are looking for predictable cash flow, well-documented systems that function without the founder, and transferable brand equity that can continue to produce value post-transaction. Ultimately, they want to reduce risk and maximize ROI. Cultural fit matters, but only if it supports long-term operational success.

On the other hand, the acquired (or the seller) is coming from a more personal perspective. They may be motivated by lifestyle change, retirement, or a desire to start a new chapter. While the financial outcome is important, so too is the reputation and the legacy. Many sellers care deeply about how their clients and their team will be treated after the deal is made and they're gone. They want a buyer who will respect what's been built, uphold cultural values, and support their people.

Recognizing these distinct priorities is essential for productive negotiation and deal-making. When both sides understand what the other truly values and communicate openly, it becomes much easier to structure an agreement that serves everyone's interests. The most successful M&A deals aren't just financial wins; they're alignment wins, rooted in mutual respect, clear expectations, and a shared vision for the future.

The Importance of Alignment

The most successful mergers and acquisitions don't begin with numbers; they begin with alignment (as you may have noticed, this is a recurring theme in this book). Long before the paperwork is signed, both parties need to examine whether they're aligned on the fundamentals, such as culture, operations, compensation structures, technology, and—most critically—vision. Consider what happens when these pieces don't line up. If one business thrives on autonomy, informal systems, and entrepreneurial freedom, while the other is driven by strict processes and centralized oversight, the post-deal integration can feel like a culture shock. Is that really such a bad thing? Yes. When you're not aligned, productivity suffers, morale dips, and good people leave.

Likewise, if one firm rewards individual performance and the other operates on team-based compensation and shared revenue, you're not just merging systems; you're also merging competing philosophies. This can naturally create friction that no integration manual can fix. That's why due diligence must go beyond legal and financial review. Yes, the numbers matter, but the operational DNA of both businesses matters more. From a buyer's perspective, the key questions to ask are:

- Are the systems built to scale, or are they overly reliant on founder intuition?

- Are team members loyal to the business or only to the founder?

- Are there term contracts in place to retain producers during the transition?

- Does the brand have value that will endure beyond the current leadership?

- How strong and efficient are the business lender relationships?

THE BUSINESS OF BROKERING

From a seller's perspective, it's just as critical to ask:

- Will your team be valued, retained, and given a platform to thrive?

- Will the company culture be respected or slowly erased?

- Will your reputation and client relationships remain intact, or be diluted?

- Will your team's perspective on lender efficiency be maintained?

Alignment isn't a nice-to-have. It's the cornerstone of any successful deal. Without it, even the most financially attractive offer can turn into a costly mistake. With it, you're not just buying or selling a business, but you're laying the groundwork for sustainable growth and shared success.

Structuring The Deal

There's no universal blueprint for structuring a merger or acquisition in the mortgage industry. Every deal is unique, shaped by the size of the businesses, the personalities involved, the financials, and the long-term goals on both sides. That said, several common structures show up again and again in the broker world.

- **Cash upfront:** The acquiring party pays a lump sum, either the full value or a significant portion, at closing. Pros? The deal is clean, simple, and preferred by sellers who want immediate liquidity. Cons? It's a higher risk for the buyer, especially if future performance is uncertain or the business is heavily dependent on its founder.

- **Earn-out:** A portion of the payment is contingent upon future performance, such as revenue, retention, or profitability milestones achieved over 12 to 60 months. Pros? It aligns incentives post-deal, and it reduces buyer risks. Cons? It can cause significant tension if performance targets are unclear or if operational changes affect results.

- **Equity swap:** Instead of cash, the seller receives equity in the acquiring company, effectively becoming a shareholder in the new, larger entity. Pros? It offers long-term upside if the acquiring firm grows, which is common in roll-up strategies. Cons? It reduces liquidity for the seller and introduces shared control dynamics.

- **Internal buyout:** Key team members, minority partners, or family members gradually purchase ownership, often funded through profit-sharing or deferred compensation. Pros? It preserves culture and continuity and can be less disruptive for the team. Cons? It requires long-term trust and often a slower payout timeline for the founder.

- **Clawback agreements:** Used when future commissions, key client retention, or broker loyalty are essential to business value. If performance dips post-sale, a portion of the payout can be reclaimed. Pros? It protects the buyer from overpaying for value that doesn't materialize. Cons? Needs very clear definitions and can cause a lot of conflict when expectations aren't aligned.

- **Hybrid structures:** Many deals combine multiple elements, such as partial cash at close, a performance-based earn-out, and a clawback provision for client attrition. The pros include that it balances risk, incentivizes performance, and creates a more flexible negotiation process.

These deals often look straightforward on paper, but the fine print matters. Even simple structures require thoughtful legal, tax, and operational planning. I highly suggest you bring in qualified legal, accounting, and M&A professionals early in the process, because a good deal isn't just about maximizing value; it's about creating clarity, avoiding surprises, and protecting relationships. In the end, the best structure is the one that reflects your goals, protects your interests, and ensures that what you've built continues to thrive.

Professional Guidance: More Than Just Legal and Financial

Most merger and acquisition transactions involve lawyers and accountants, and rightly so. Legal structure, tax implications, and due diligence are all essential components of any deal. However, in the mortgage industry, where the business is driven by people, relationships, and intricate operations, standard professional support is often insufficient. Structuring a deal that truly works in practice and not just on paper requires guidance from people who understand the inner workings of a brokerage. For example, they must understand:

- How compensation models impact retention

- What drives client and referral partner loyalty

- Why cultural integration can make or break a transition

- Where operational blind spots are likely to appear

That's why many brokerage owners turn to strategic advisors who have walked in their shoes, including individuals or firms that have built, scaled, and exited mortgage businesses and understand the human, operational, and emotional dynamics involved. One such example is my company, Adlam Advisory Group. It was created specifically to support business owners through the complexities of buying, selling, or partnering in the mortgage space with a focus on aligning structure with strategy. Their role goes beyond term sheets and valuations. They help leaders:

- Preserve the integrity of the brand and culture

- Protect key team members and referral pipelines

- Craft deal terms that support long-term value, not just short-term wins

- Stay grounded in the vision that made the business successful in the first place

Whether you're acquiring another brokerage, exploring a strategic partnership, or preparing for your own eventual exit, having a seasoned guide at the table can be the difference between a deal that simply closes and one that truly succeeds. Legal and financial experts will help navigate contracts, compliance, and valuation, which is essential work, but it's the strategic insight from someone who understands the mortgage industry from the inside out that ensures the deal is not only sound but also sustainable. They will help you see around corners, anticipate integration challenges, and make decisions that protect both the business and the people behind it.

The Role of the Leader

Another aspect of any merger or acquisition that shouldn't be overlooked but often is, is the role of the existing leadership team post-transaction. In many deals, particularly when brokers are not bound by long-term agreements or when a large number of contracts are nearing expiration, the acquiring party will normally insist that the principal broker or owner remain involved, typically for a transitional period of three to five years. This continuity helps ensure stability, maintains client and team confidence, and allows time for trust to shift from the founder to the new leadership structure.

If the business is highly dependent on the personality, relationships, or presence of its founder, an abrupt exit can create disruption or even trigger an exodus of brokers and clients. Conversely, if the business has been built with institutional readiness in mind, with strong systems, documented processes, distributed leadership, and a well-embedded culture, the transition can happen more quickly and smoothly. In cases where the business is being passed on to internal successors, such as existing team members or minority shareholders, the most effective leaders begin preparing well in advance. They delegate authority, mentor rising leaders, and make strategic space for others to lead well before the legal transfer of ownership. In this way, leadership isn't just handed off, but developed over time.

This is the heart of effective succession planning. When done intentionally, it doesn't just support a smoother transition. It also increases the confidence of buyers, reduces risk, and ultimately boosts the value and long-term viability of the business.

Red Flags and Warning Signs

While mergers, acquisitions, and partnerships can be powerful growth tools, they can also expose your business to serious risk if not approached with caution. Whether you're buying, selling, or exploring a partnership, it's essential to look beyond the surface and assess the structural integrity of the business. Here are some common red flags to watch for:

- **Lack of Clear Broker Agreements or IP Ownership:** If there are weak contracts with brokers or if ownership of intellectual property (like branding, marketing materials, or proprietary systems) isn't clearly documented, you may be inheriting uncertainty. This makes it harder to retain talent, protect assets, or ensure operational continuity.

- **Poor CRM or Deal Tracking:** A disorganized or outdated customer relationship management system is a sign of inefficiency and a lack of scalability. If deals are being tracked manually, inconsistently, or not at all, it becomes difficult to validate performance and predict future revenue. If team members are using different CRMs, this is also not ideal.

- **No Clarity on Revenue Sharing or Compensation Structures:** When compensation models are vague, inconsistent, or overly reliant on informal agreements, disputes can quickly arise post-transaction. A well-structured revenue-sharing plan should be transparent, enforceable, and aligned with business goals.

- **Founder-Centric Decision Making:** If the business still revolves entirely around the founder, meaning they're the only one making decisions, holding client relationships, or resolving internal issues, the risk is high. Without decentralized leadership, the business may struggle to survive their departure.

- **Hidden Liabilities or Legal Disputes:** Always conduct thorough due diligence to uncover any unresolved legal issues, tax liabilities, compliance violations, or regulatory red flags. These hidden landmines can surface long after a deal is signed and lead to significant financial or reputational damage.

M&A success isn't just about spotting the opportunity, but also about knowing what to avoid. When in doubt, slow down, ask tough questions, and bring in experienced advisors who can help you see what others might miss. The best deals are built on transparency, preparation, and aligned expectations, not urgency or emotion. M&A can be a tremendous opportunity, but only if approached with clarity, patience, and a long-term lens. Institutional readiness isn't just about systems; it's about leadership, contracts, and transferability of trust. So, be sure that's what you're working toward.

Free Download: M&A 101 Guide—10 Things to Know Before You Merge or Buy

For a free downloadable guide outlining the fundamentals of mergers, acquisitions, and partnerships, go to: dougadlam.com/brokering

Or scan the QR code below:

Chapter 18

Risks, Liabilities, and Lawsuits

If there's one thing no one likes to talk about (but every good business owner must), it's the topic of risk. In this industry, risk isn't limited to rate volatility, market downturns, or economic cycles. The more dangerous threats are often the ones you don't see coming: overlooked compliance steps, inadequate documentation, misaligned incentives, poor internal processes, or a single misstep by someone on your team. One signature in the wrong place, one conversation that wasn't properly disclosed, one client who feels misled—that's all it takes for risk to become liability and for liability to escalate into a lawsuit.

Risk in a mortgage business is complex because it comes from multiple directions: legal, reputational, operational, regulatory, and interpersonal. The real challenge isn't just responding to issues as they arise, but proactively designing your business to minimize exposure in the first place. This chapter is about the unglamorous but critical work of protecting what you've built. You'll hear real-world stories of what happens when things go sideways, and what strong leaders do to respond. Ultimately, you'll see that risk management isn't just a back-office function; it's a front-line leadership responsibility.

The Hidden Risks in Broker Businesses

In the mortgage business, the most dangerous risks are rarely the obvious ones. They don't always show up as red flags or dramatic moments. More often, they hide in the cracks of your daily operations, such as small oversights, outdated practices, or unclear expectations that quietly accumulate until something breaks. Some of the biggest threats to your business are buried in the routine:

- Brokers operating without signed or up-to-date agreements

- Compliance processes that vary from person to person, or don't exist at all

- Inconsistent documentation, missing notes, or poor use of your CRM

- Team members exceeding the scope of their role or license

- Failure to properly update clients on product terms, conditions, and risks

- Leaders with no insight into the satisfaction or experience of clients that their brokers have served

- Brokers giving poor or self-serving advice, or worse, committing fraud without leadership's knowledge (e.g., falsifying income documents, misrepresenting facts to lenders)

These aren't theoretical risks. They're real issues that have caused real damage to reputations, to client trust, to regulatory standing, and to business continuity. The danger is that they rarely feel urgent until it's too late. Hidden risks tend to reveal themselves in three ways: client complaints, regulatory scrutiny, or lawsuits. Usually, by the time they show up in any of those forms, your ability to contain the fallout is significantly reduced.

So, what can you do about it? The best thing you can do is to have risk management plans. What do I mean by risk management? In my books, risk management isn't just about having insurance or reacting when something goes wrong. It's about building a business where the right guardrails are in place from the start, so that risk has fewer places to hide.

Legal Foundations to Build Early

In the mortgage business, your contracts are more than paperwork; they're your first and most reliable line of defense. Solid legal foundations safeguard your reputation, finances, relationships, and future options. Yet, many broker-owners treat legal infrastructure as a "later" investment, or just do the bare minimum, revisiting it only when something has gone wrong. To avoid this happening or sneaking up on you when it's too late to do something about it, here are some legal foundations that every brokerage should prioritize and build from the start.

- **Broker Agreements:** Whether with or without fixed terms, these agreements should clearly outline expectations, responsibilities, compensation, exit clauses, and intellectual property protections. This helps avoid disputes and misalignment down the road.

- **Team Member Roles and Expectations:** Clearly define roles, reporting structures, scope of license, and performance benchmarks. If you leave it vague, you invite confusion and, in some cases, liability.

- **Policies and Procedures Manual:** This outlines the operating procedures, such as compliance, communication, and complaint handling, that must be followed by all licensed and unlicensed team members.

- **Client-Facing Agreements:** Tools like an Agreement of Understanding can set clear expectations around service, obligations, and decision-making authority. This protects both the client experience and your business.

- **Proper Disclosures:** Templated disclosures are not enough. Every deal is different, and your documentation should reflect that. Customize disclosures to match the nuances of the file, the product, and the risk.

It's tempting to delay legal spending, especially in the early stages when budgets are tight. However, investing in strong contracts is a fraction of the cost (financial, emotional, and reputational) of defending yourself in court, dealing with regulators, or trying to repair a broken partnership. But remember, legal work isn't a one-and-done exercise. As your business grows, so do your risks. What protected you when you had two brokers, likely won't hold up when you have twenty. Make it a regular leadership habit to revisit your legal infrastructure, including contracts, clauses, and liability shields, any time your business model evolves, your team expands, or the regulatory environment shifts. At the end of the day, building a sellable business starts with building a defendable one.

Errors and Omissions Insurance: More Than a Policy

Errors and Omissions (E&O) insurance is more than just a regulatory checkbox. It's a business-critical layer of protection. Yet, too often, brokers and brokerage leaders misunderstand what it truly covers, what it doesn't, and how it functions in practice. Let's start with the basics: Not all E&O policies are created equal. If your business engages in private lending, commercial transactions, or broker-led underwriting, you're operating in higher-risk territory. If you have brokers lending out their own money, this opens a whole different can of worms for E&O providers, and many will not insure your brokerage if anyone is lending out their own funds. These activities often carry exclusions, higher deductibles, or increased premiums. If your current policy doesn't specifically cover these exposures, you may be leaving yourself and your team vulnerable. Here are a few additional points to consider regarding E&O insurance.

The Illusion of Blanket Coverage

Many brokers working under a brokerage umbrella assume they're fully protected by the parent brokerage's E&O policy. But here's the truth: Most brokerages build their own legal shields into policy. Their coverage is structured to protect the brokerage and not just the brokers. If a broker's actions deviate from the company's written policies and procedures, even just slightly, those deviations can be used as grounds to deny coverage, shift liability, or pass legal costs down to the individual broker. This isn't malicious; it's structural. Brokerages include clauses in their manuals, training materials, and contracts that state: "If you don't follow the rules, we're not on the hook for your mistakes."

As a leader, it's your responsibility to ensure your team knows what those rules are and that they actually follow them. This means more than handing over a manual. It includes active mentorship, proper onboarding, regular training, ongoing supervision, and operational clarity. Protecting your people isn't just about buying insurance; it's about building a culture of competence and compliance.

The Shifting Role of Brokerages

When you look closely, you'll see that there's a broader business trend playing out here. With tighter margins and competitive commission splits, many brokerages have made a conscious decision to reduce their role as a protector. Legal exposure is expensive. Some have shifted toward a "support-only" model, offering compliance tools, training, and coaching, but distancing themselves from liability when brokers fall short. The reason? Economics. A low-margin brokerage can't afford to take on the risk. So it restructures its contracts to hold brokers more accountable, and itself less accountable. While most regulators will ultimately hold the brokerage responsible for compliance breaches, many brokerages will pursue cost recovery through broker contracts, including legal fees.

I'm not saying this in a negative light. This isn't about criticizing any one model. Rather, it's about clarity and informed decision-making. Every business structure comes with trade-offs. Just like no-frills mortgage products offer lower rates with fewer features and expensive penalty clauses, low-split brokerage models often provide less protection and oversight. If you're opting for a model that gives you maximum autonomy and maximum split, know what you're giving up. If you're leading a team, make sure your policies, procedures, and insurance truly match the level of risk you're taking on. Because when things go wrong, and at some point they will, it's not just about who's insured. It's about who's prepared.

Culture of Compliance

One important shift to make is to stop seeing compliance as just a set of rules and to begin embracing it as a mindset. In a mortgage business, compliance can't be restricted to one department or one desk. It has to be part of your culture. When brokers treat compliance as a tedious checkbox exercise, risk rises. Corners get cut, details are missed, and that's when mistakes happen. I'm not talking administrative slip-ups here, but serious regulatory breaches, client complaints, and even legal consequences. When compliance is understood as a protective tool—something that safeguards the broker, client, and reputation of the business—it becomes empowering. It's no longer just about staying out of trouble but about doing the right thing, the right way, every time.

So, how can you do that? To build a true culture of compliance, it must be embedded into the everyday rhythm of your business. That includes:

- **Onboarding:** During onboarding, you should not only introduce the rules but also explain why they matter.

- **Training:** When training occurs, it should include real-world scenarios and grey zones, not just policy reviews.

- **Team huddles and check-ins:** When you have team huddles and check-ins, include space to address compliance questions or updates.

- **Success stories:** Don't keep your team in the dark about the success of compliance. Highlight not only top sales, but top conduct. For example, honor brokers who navigated tricky situations with integrity, or actively monitor and reward compliance efficiency within your team in the form of a KPI (for example, the ratio of files submitted with no compliance errors to the total number of files submitted to compliance).

The goal is to normalize discussing compliance by making it a regular topic of conversation, rather than one that only arises when something goes wrong. Treat it as a source of confidence and professionalism, not fear. As the leader, your attitude toward compliance sets the tone for your team. If you dismiss it as paperwork, your brokers will follow suit. But if you lead with accountability, ask good questions, and model ethical decision-making, that becomes the standard. In the end, a culture of compliance doesn't slow down your business, but protects and strengthens it by building trust from the inside out.

Internal SOPs: Your Safety Net and Success Strategy

Whether you're leading a brokerage, operating a sub-brokerage, managing a team, or working as a solo broker with support staff, you are running a business. And every successful business runs on systems. Standard Operating Procedures (SOPs) are often misunderstood as bureaucratic paperwork or just another compliance chore. In reality, they're the backbone of an efficient, consistent, and lower-risk operation. SOPs aren't just about ticking boxes for regulators. They perform multiple functions:

- Aligning your team around common expectations and workflows

- Ensuring clients receive a consistent experience, regardless of who serves them

- Reducing training time and knowledge gaps when new team members join

- Preventing errors, missed steps, and miscommunication

- Serving as critical documentation in the event of a dispute, audit, or legal claim

Strong SOPs don't need to be complicated, but they must be clear, repeatable, and accessible. Focus on the high-impact workflows that touch your clients, lenders, and regulatory responsibilities. These typically include:

- Client onboarding

- Document collection

- Lender recommendation

- Application submission

- Follow-up

- Condition collection

- Pre-funding audits

- Post-closing communications

- File storage

- Referral asks

Each of these processes should have a defined set of steps, assigned responsibilities, expected timelines, and clear escalation paths in place in case something goes off track. When your business runs on well-defined SOPs, you reduce your dependency on any one person, including yourself. That means fewer operational risks, faster onboarding, easier delegation, and more seamless cross-coverage in case of illness or vacation, resulting in a business that is far more appealing to lenders, partners, customers, and future buyers. In short, SOPs make your business safer, smoother, and more valuable. They're your safety net when things go wrong and your success strategy when you're ready to grow.

When Things Go Wrong

Even the most buttoned-up, well-run businesses will eventually face a complaint, a compliance investigation, or the threat of legal action. It's not a question of if; it's a question of when. When that moment comes, your ability to respond quickly, calmly, and strategically will define the outcome. So, how does one prepare for things to go wrong? Here are four steps to help you manage a crisis effectively.

Step 1: Have a Communication Plan

The first few hours of a crisis are critical and can make or break your business. To ensure success within the first few hours, you need a clear internal protocol. Who handles client communication? Who interfaces with regulators, lenders, or stakeholders? Who coordinates internal escalation and documentation review? Having answers to these questions will allow you to act without emotion but with urgency, as you'll have an appointed leader and crisis manager. It's vital for the rest of your team to be aware of who is in charge to avoid conflict within the crisis.

Step 2: Centralize Documentation

Your best defence is always your documentation. Ensure your CRM (or file management system) contains a comprehensive record of client communication, including all required disclosures and signed agreements, as well as internal notes on advice provided, changes requested, or concerns raised. Some broker operations take this as far as recording all phone calls. If your documentation is disorganized, fragmented, or incomplete, your risk increases exponentially. Regulators and courts won't just evaluate what you say happened; they'll ask what you can prove.

Step 3: Stay Calm and Solution-Focused

Panic leads to poor decisions. Escalate the situation internally first, before issuing statements or responses externally. Avoid placing blame or getting defensive. Instead, start by gathering facts, reviewing the timeline, determining the severity and the stakeholders involved, and deciding whether the issue is isolated or systemic. Approach the situation as an opportunity to resolve, learn, and reinforce your commitment to professionalism and compliance.

Step 4: Engage the Right Professionals Early

Don't wait until things spiral out of control before involving professionals. Here are the four most important people you should involve:

- **Lawyer:** To understand your legal exposure and options

- **Compliance officer:** To ensure alignment with industry regulations

- **Insurance provider:** Particularly if your E&O policy may apply

- **Crisis PR advisor:** If there's media interest or brand risk involved

These professionals can help shape your messaging, protect your interests, and often, de-escalate what initially feels unmanageable. Crises are inevitable, but chaos isn't. With a plan in place, clear documentation, and the right advisors at your side, even the worst-case scenarios can be contained and, in some cases, turned into long-term credibility builders.

Lessons From the Trenches

Sometimes the most expensive mistakes aren't made out of malice or negligence. Rather, they're made in the margins, the quick decisions, the assumed understandings, and the shortcuts taken during busy seasons. Over the years, I've seen both individual brokers and entire businesses face serious consequences because of:

- Miscommunications around rate holds that weren't clearly documented

- Verbal promises made by brokers that never made it into writing

- Clients' misunderstanding prepayment penalties and holding the broker accountable

- Private mortgages with vague terms and poor documentation

- Conditions being waived prematurely, with clients later claiming the broker told them to proceed

In nearly every case, the root cause wasn't intentional wrongdoing. It was weak documentation, inconsistent processes, poorly communicated expectations, and ultimately, a breakdown in leadership oversight. There's one specific story that still sticks with me. Years after funding a deal, I had to write a significant cheque to a long-time client. Why? Because our internal process missed a critical product term. Both our team and the client believed the mortgage was a standard product. Only years later did we discover it was actually a no-frills mortgage, with a significantly higher penalty formula.

Could I have blamed the lender? Maybe. Could I have pointed fingers at our team? Sure. Could I have argued that the client signed the paperwork? Absolutely. But at the end of the day, the responsibility was mine. Our systems weren't tight enough, our process left too much room for assumption, and because I value long-term trust more than short-term savings, I wrote the cheque. That moment reshaped how I thought about compliance: not as bureaucracy or red tape, but as a form of protection. Protection for our clients, our team, our business, our reputation, and my peace of mind.

The best brokers don't just avoid mistakes; they build systems that make mistakes nearly impossible. And when the unexpected happens, they own it, because leadership isn't just about growth, it's also about accountability.

Risk is a Leadership Responsibility

Risk doesn't live in the compliance department. It lives at the top with you. As a business owner, team lead, or managing broker, your job isn't just to drive volume or recruit talent. Your job is to protect what you've built. That means understanding that risk management is not a delegated task; it's a core part of your leadership DNA. Too often, leaders view risk as someone else's department or something they'll "deal with if it comes up." But that mindset is what turns manageable issues into existential threats. Real leadership means being proactive about the vulnerabilities inside your business.

Risk management isn't just about avoiding lawsuits or regulatory complaints. It's about building a business that's resilient, reputable, and ready for growth. Because your business is only as strong as its weakest link, and your legal, reputational, and operational risk is only as low as the worst-case scenario you've prepared for. So, build for growth, lead with integrity, and protect your downside. That's not just compliance; that's innovative entrepreneurship.

Free Download: Business Risk Assessment

For a free downloadable assessment to identify risks, gaps, and vulnerabilities within your business—and highlight areas needing immediate attention, go to: dougadlam.com/brokering

Or scan the QR code below:

Chapter 19

What the Industry Needs Next

Every industry needs to evolve; otherwise, it will get left behind. Mortgage brokering is no exception to this rule. We're currently at a pivotal moment where legacy systems, outdated mindsets, and fractured approaches are beginning to show their cracks. To ensure long-term viability and relevance, brokerages, networks, lenders, technology suppliers, and other key industry partners must do more than just keep up. They must also anticipate, adapt, and act.

Currently, the market is shifting, consumer expectations are rising, regulations are tightening, and technology is moving faster than most operators are prepared for, and so are the fraudsters. What worked a decade ago is no longer enough to compete, much less to lead. But this chapter isn't about trends. Trends come and go, but imperatives allow you to evolve. From my perspective, there are a few things we need as an industry, which is exactly what we'll discuss in this chapter, starting with banking and AI.

Smarter Use of Open Banking and AI

Canada is still playing catch-up when it comes to open banking, but it won't be for long. The regulatory wheels are in motion, and once consumer-permissioned data sharing becomes mainstream, the mortgage industry will feel the impact overnight. Brokers who are prepared will thrive, while those who aren't will scramble to keep up. There are two main areas that everyone in the industry should be prepared for: open banking and artificial intelligence.

Open Banking enables clients to securely share their financial data, like bank account histories, income, and liabilities, with approved third parties, including brokers and lenders. This has the power to radically simplify the mortgage process. It means instant access to verified income and spending patterns, faster underwriting and approval decisions, reduced paperwork, less back-and-forth with clients, and improved accuracy, reducing human error and risk.

At the same time, AI and automation are no longer "coming soon." They're already embedded in leading broker businesses. Whether it's AI-driven lead nurturing, chatbot-assisted client communication, predictive analytics for deal structuring, or automated compliance pre-checks, these tools can save time, reduce risk, and increase conversion. But here's the catch: These technologies are only as good as the people using them. To effectively use AI, leaders must learn how to evaluate AI solutions, train teams to adopt new tools responsibly and ethically, stay aware of privacy laws and usage boundaries, and recognize where automation adds value and where the human touch is still essential.

Despite what many think, these technologies won't replace brokers. The human touch is still necessary. But brokers who embrace them and learn to lead with them will absolutely replace those who don't. Technology now allows brokers to do on average three times as many mortgage files in the same time as five years ago, and AI is adding additional efficiency to the process. Despite the fact that underwriting continues to become more challenging, and brokers often find themselves fighting for every deal, the reality is that fewer brokers will end up doing more deals. Those who don't adapt and lead will lose. Those who choose to accept the evolution will win.

Tighter Fraud Prevention

Fraud in the mortgage industry is no longer limited to the occasional forged document. Today's bad actors are using advanced tactics like synthetic identities, deepfake documentation, and digital manipulation to slip through outdated systems. Unfortunately, the industry's fraud prevention mechanisms haven't evolved fast enough to meet the threat. We need more than awareness and infrastructure to achieve better fraud prevention.

What we really need is advanced documentation verification tools that can detect tampering beyond the naked eye, as well as a shared fraud database across broker networks, lenders, and insurers to flag bad actors. Additionally, the industry can also do with some enhanced, comprehensive broker training on spotting red flags, escalation protocols, and compliance procedures. The key to success lies in real collaboration between all players in the mortgage ecosystem, which includes lenders, insurers, brokerages, tech providers, regulators, and associations.

The good news is that Open Banking and automation offer a path forward. With secure, direct access to banking records, CRA documents, and financial statements, brokers and lenders can validate income and assets in real time. This will drastically reduce opportunities for falsification and improve both speed and accuracy. But technology isn't the only issue. Culture is also a major factor.

The quiet exit of bad actors continues to haunt the industry, and it's a systematic failure in my opinion. When brokers or bankers are caught submitting fraudulent documents or misleading clients, too many are allowed to quietly resign. No record. No accountability. Weeks later, they resurface at another bank, brokerage, or lender, free to repeat the behavior. In many cases, regulators are never informed, and misconduct goes unreported. This revolving door must be closed. We need clear, consistent protocols for reporting unethical or fraudulent behavior, communicating issues across brokerages and lenders, and supporting whistleblowers without fear of retaliation.

The truth is, fraud doesn't just hurt one lender or client. It also undermines trust across the entire industry. Silence, no matter how well-intentioned, protects no one. So, let's change it.

Regulatory Consistency and Clarity

Canada's provincial regulatory frameworks are often misaligned, and for brokers who operate in more than one province, this creates unnecessary complexity and risk. From licensing requirements to client disclosures, the rules can differ just enough to create confusion, inconsistency, or even non-compliance. The industry needs better national alignment in key areas, including:

- **Licensing requirements:** To allow brokers to scale operations without navigating entirely different rulebooks.

- **Continuing education standards:** So professional development is meaningful and transferable.

- **Disclosure language, terminology, and timing:** To ensure consumers receive consistent information, regardless of location.

Beyond consistency, we also need clarity, and that starts with regulators gaining a better understanding of how modern mortgage businesses actually function. Too often, policies are crafted based on outdated assumptions or legacy brokerage models that no longer reflect the reality of today's hybrid, virtual, or tech-enabled teams. Well-intentioned rules can quickly become barriers when they fail to account for how the industry has evolved.

To move forward, we need more open dialogue between regulators, industry leaders, and associations across the country. We also need policy development informed by real-world business models and a shift from reactive enforcement to proactive collaboration. Think about it like this: Consistency and clarity don't mean lowering standards. They mean raising the bar together.

Broker Licensing Standards

One of the mortgage industry's greatest vulnerabilities is also one of its entry points: the licensing process. The bar to becoming a mortgage broker remains too low in many provinces, and that has real consequences for clients, businesses, and the industry's credibility. Becoming a real estate agent, certified financial planner, or accountant requires significant investment in time, coursework, and examination. In contrast, many provinces allow individuals to become licensed mortgage brokers with minimal training, despite the fact that brokers help clients take on the largest financial obligation of their lives. And yet, the income potential for mortgage brokers often matches or exceeds that of other professions. So why is the educational bar so much lower?

To be clear, this isn't about gatekeeping. It's about responsibility. We must raise the standard for education and licensing, build robust continuing education programs that go beyond compliance refreshers, and develop leadership, business, and risk management training for those scaling. The goal is not to exclude, but to elevate. Stronger education leads to better advice, reduced fraud, and more sustainable businesses. It creates a generation of brokers who are prepared not just to transact, but to lead. If we want to be taken seriously as financial professionals, we need to act like it, starting from day one.

Broker Business Education

Most brokers enter the industry because they want to help clients, not necessarily to build companies. But the moment a broker hires a team, forms a sub-brokerage, or opens their own brokerage, they step into an entirely different role: entrepreneur. Yet, we don't set them up to succeed in that role. There's a major gap in business education within the mortgage industry. Brokers are often left to figure out complex leadership, operational, and compliance challenges on their own, learning through trial and error, sometimes at great cost to their business, their clients, or their reputation.

If we want brokers to thrive beyond the transaction, we need to support them in becoming strong business leaders. That means providing:

- Training in core business competencies like financial literacy, operational systems, regulatory compliance, and leadership

- Coaching programs designed to support sustainable, long-term growth

- Strategic resources for scaling, including succession planning, technology adoption, and team development

Licensing may open the door, but it doesn't prepare brokers to run businesses. If we want a stronger, more resilient industry, we need to close that gap and make business education a standard, not a luxury. Because the most successful brokers of the future won't just know how to structure a mortgage, they'll know how to build and lead enduring businesses.

Collaboration Over Competition

We often say we're part of a broker community, but too frequently, we act like we're competing in separate silos. The truth is, the brokers and leaders who thrive long-term are rarely the most secretive. They're the ones who share openly, mentor generously, and believe that rising tides lift all boats. They understand that protecting "trade secrets" doesn't build an industry; it builds walls. As a profession, we need to move beyond scarcity thinking and start cultivating real collaboration. That means:

- Creating spaces for mastermind groups where brokers can exchange ideas, strategies, and challenges without fear of competition

- Sharing best practices publicly, especially when it comes to compliance, client experience, technology, and leadership

- Investing in mentorship and talent development, helping new brokers learn the ropes faster and with fewer missteps

A stronger, more trusted industry isn't built in isolation. It's built through conversation, contribution, and collective growth. When done right, collaboration doesn't dilute your success; it multiplies it.

Purposeful Signing Bonuses

One of the more curious developments in the Canadian mortgage industry is the increasing prevalence of signing bonuses. These are upfront lump-sum payments offered to brokerages, sub-brokerages, broker teams, and even individual brokers when they commit to a new network or brand, typically in exchange for a specific commission split over a set contract term. In essence, it's a partial "exit" without a full departure. You stay in the game, but you cash in a portion of your chips early. These agreements are almost always confidential, quietly negotiated between leadership and the parent organization. But while a signing bonus can feel like a windfall, it's not free money. It's capital with conditions, and its strategic use (or misuse) can either strengthen or fracture the foundation of your business.

So, what's the purpose of a signing bonus? If it can do more harm than good, why are so many mortgage businesses adopting it as part of their business model? Well, if used well, a signing bonus can be more than just a payday. It can help solve real problems, offset real costs, and support meaningful transitions. Here are some of the common and practical uses:

- **Offsetting time and effort:** Changing brokerages is not a light lift. It requires research, meetings, contract negotiations, and plenty of administrative heavy lifting. As both a principal broker and a former Director of Growth for a national brokerage, I've seen the strain this puts on leadership and support teams. A signing bonus can act as compensation for the sheer volume of work involved.

- **Rebranding and co-branding costs:** Switching networks often means updating everything from signage and websites to social media, email, and print materials. It's not just about money, but about a drain on your time, energy, and creativity. A signing bonus can help fund that transition.

- **Lender credentialing and onboarding:** Moving brokerages frequently involves acquiring new lender credentials, navigating portal setups, and retraining teams on different processes. This transition can temporarily disrupt operations, and the bonus helps soften that impact.

- **Growth strategy via structured loan:** Some leaders treat the bonus as a form of creative financing, using it to fund new offices, renovations, marketing campaigns, events, or recruiting efforts. In these cases, the slightly lower commission split acts like a loan repayment over the term.

- **Debt paydown:** In some cases, bonuses can be used to stabilize the business by paying down debts from over-expansion, missed incentives, legal costs, or just keeping the lights on during a tough cycle. It's a reset button, but it should be pressed with intention.

Like many other things in this industry, every signing bonus comes with strings. Most often, they include limitations such as minimum volume thresholds, exclusive platform usage, fixed terms, leadership commitments, reduced commission splits, and transferability clauses. Understanding these terms and their long-term impact is critical. These small prints also lead to a bigger question: If signing bonuses are a viable strategy if done intentionally, who should receive a bonus?

This is where things can get complicated and political. The bonus is often paid to the business or ownership group. But top-producing agents, whose volume helped secure the deal, may feel entitled to a share. If they find out about a bonus they weren't told about or included in, trust can erode fast, and culture can unravel even faster. So, who should actually get the bonus? The answer lies in a few key questions: Who built the brand, team, and systems? Who negotiated the deals? Who bears the legal and financial risk? Who is contractually tied to the agreement? At the end of the day, leadership must decide how best to use the funds for the health and greater good of the business. That might mean debt repayment, brand upgrades, tech improvements, or team expansion— and not personal payouts. While NDAs may limit what you can share, transparency wherever possible is critical, as secrecy breeds suspicion.

What the industry needs is for everyone to start asking strategic questions before accepting any signing bonus. Here are some example questions:

- Is this a strategic investment or a short-term band-aid?

- Will this bonus be used to grow the business, or just keep it afloat?

- Are you trading long-term control and equity for a short-term cash injection?

- Would you be better off with a more favourable split and no bonus?

- Can the bonus be reinvested in ways that benefit the whole team?

At the end of the day, a signing bonus is neither good nor bad. It's simply a tool, and like any tool, its impact depends on how and why you use it. Approached with clarity and strategy, a signing bonus can accelerate your next chapter. Misused, it can create resentment, conflict, and long-term constraints. The key is being honest with yourself and your team (where permitted), and making sure the decision aligns with your bigger vision. Use it to build. Not to patch.

The Future Isn't Coming. It's Here

The mortgage industry isn't waiting for change; it's already in motion. Technology is advancing, client expectations are shifting, competition is rising, and regulatory pressures are evolving. The question is no longer *if* we'll adapt, but *how quickly*. We can't rely on others to lead the charge. It's up to all of us—brokers, lenders, tech innovators, educators, associations, and industry leaders—to shape what comes next. Waiting on the sidelines isn't a strategy. It's a risk.

The businesses that will thrive in the next decade are those that embrace innovation without losing sight of human connection, build resilient, adaptive cultures rooted in trust, prioritize client experience at every stage, and invest in continuous learning and team empowerment.

The future of mortgage brokering in Canada isn't a distant concept. It's already here, and it's being shaped by the decisions we make today. So, don't just prepare for it. Lead it.

Free Download: Industry Evolution Worksheet

For a free downloadable worksheet to brainstorm how the industry can evolve—and identify the opportunities that will best position your business for the future, go to: dougadlam.com/brokering

Or scan the QR code below:

Chapter 20

What's Your Legacy?

When you think about your possible legacy, what comes to mind? What do you want to leave behind when you step away? Do you want to be remembered as the broker with the fanciest car on the block? Or perhaps that broker with the large billboards and perfect smile? Maybe it's none of that. Maybe you want to leave behind good finances or be remembered as a good boss who helped others create success. Well, whether you've thought about it or not, we're all building a legacy. The question isn't whether or not you'll leave a legacy behind; it's more about what that legacy will be.

Legacy in the mortgage industry isn't just about how long you've been in the business or how well you're known. It's about what you leave behind when you're no longer at the helm. It's about whether your business can thrive without you, whether your clients are served well in your absence, and whether your systems and brand have real, transferable value. A true legacy isn't built on personal heroics. It's built on repeatable processes, empowered people, and a clear vision that extends beyond the founder. It's the difference between owning a job and owning a business.

This final chapter will explore what it means to create a lasting legacy. One that frees you from day-to-day dependency, enables meaningful growth, and provides a path to eventual succession or sale. At the end of the day, your legacy isn't just the deals you close; it's the infrastructure, independence, and impact you build along the way.

The Myth of Indispensability

As we know by now, many mortgage professionals unknowingly build businesses that rely entirely on their personal involvement. Every client interaction, decision, and relationship runs through one person: them. In the early years, this level of control may feel efficient or even necessary, but over time, it becomes a bottleneck. Being indispensable might feel like job security, but in reality, it's a liability. It limits your ability to scale, step away, or sell. You may be the reason your business grew, using your expertise, reputation, and hustle, but you cannot be the reason it can't survive or thrive without you.

If your business only works when you're in the room, you're not building something with a worthy legacy. Real legacy begins when you shift from being essential to being optional, and when you build systems, delegate authority, and empower others to carry the mission forward.

Scale Without You

Building a legacy-worthy business isn't easy, especially if you're used to running the show. Oftentimes, professionals believe that in order to create a legacy, you need to create something with your name, but that's not the case. True legacy is creating something that outlives you. Even if your name is forgotten, the positive effect of your actions will continue to live on. A legacy-worthy business is defined by how well it can run without you. That doesn't mean that you're not valuable, but it does mean that you've invested more into building a structure than fanning an ego.

A sellable business is one that will carry a legacy because it's one where you're developing roles, responsibilities, and processes that allow your team to deliver consistent results without your day-to-day involvement. You've turned your knowledge into systems and empowered others to execute. So, don't view your business and legacy as a vanity project to make your name known. See it as an opportunity to plant seeds that will grow into trees that will stand long after you're gone.

The Value of Client Independence

In the early stages of a mortgage business, it's natural for clients to associate the experience and the trust with you personally. Your name is the brand. But if your long-term goal is to build a business that has value beyond you, that must change. Client loyalty needs to shift from the individual to the institution. That transition only happens when every client, regardless of who manages their file, receives the same level of care, clarity, and confidence.

This is where your systems, processes, and people come in. A repeatable, high-quality experience creates consistency, consistency builds trust, and trust in your business, instead of just in you, is what ultimately drives brand equity and business valuation. When clients say, "I trust your team" instead of "I only trust you," you know you're building something with legacy potential.

When clients are dependent on your business, instead of on you personally, something magical happens: you experience freedom. When clients are dependent on you, it can quickly get uncomfortable and lead to burnout. But when they rely on your business and your team, it creates a healthy ecosystem.

When I first stepped back from day-to-day operations, I expected to feel anxious. But instead, I felt free and liberated. I realized then that my greatest value wasn't doing the deals myself, but designing a business that could deliver exceptional outcomes without me. When the team could operate independently, it didn't diminish my role; it amplified the business's worth. Removing myself from the daily grind created space for growth, not just for me but for everyone around me.

This is the true power of building a business that doesn't revolve around you: It multiplies your impact, increases your options, and gives you your time back. Client dependency might feel validating in the moment, but freedom, scale, and legacy live on the other side of it.

When You Don't Have a Choice

We often frame the idea of building a self-sustaining business around freedom: freedom to travel, to innovate, to spend more time with loved ones, or to pursue new ventures. While that's a compelling vision, there's another, far less glamorous reason to build a business that runs without you: What happens when you don't have a choice?

Life is unpredictable, and emergencies don't wait for your pipeline to clear. Family crises don't coordinate with your quarter-end, and burnout doesn't ask for permission before it knocks you off your feet. Over the years, I've seen top-producing brokers and business owners forced to step away from their companies for reasons no business plan accounted for:

- A sudden cancer diagnosis or major surgery

- Physical or emotional burnout from years of nonstop hustle

- Becoming the primary caregiver for an aging parent or a sick child

- The birth or adoption of a child without adequate time to prepare

- Grieving the loss of a loved one—and the logistical weight that comes with it

- Being named executor or power of attorney, which becomes an all-consuming role

- Personal or professional legal complications

- Emergency relocations due to family immigration or cross-border commitments

- Natural disasters like wildfires, floods, or ice storms that bring business to a standstill

- Divorce or relationship breakdowns with far-reaching financial, mental health, and operational impacts

- Death

In each of these cases, the ability to protect the business and its value came down to what was in place before the crisis hit. Systems, people, and processes are shock absorbers, not just efficiency tools. That's why we don't just build for some distant "someday" like retirement, the sale, or the five-year plan. We build for optionality and resilience because when life throws a curveball, legacy isn't just about reputation. It's about ensuring your business can stand and serve without you. Designing for legacy is designing for life, and sometimes, life doesn't give you a choice.

Who Are You Letting Down by Not Building a Sellable Business?

Building a business that depends entirely on you doesn't just restrict your freedom or affect a possible legacy; it also creates risk for everyone around you. When you choose not to design a company that can function and grow without your constant involvement, the consequences ripple far beyond your own life. You're not just limiting your options; you may also be letting people down.

Your family counts on the business for financial security, stability, and time with you. If the business collapses the moment you step away, they carry the weight of that fallout. Your team has chosen to build their careers with you. They rely on your vision, infrastructure, and planning to create long-term growth. If your business can't stand without you, their jobs and futures are at risk. And your clients trust your brand during one of the most significant financial decisions of their lives. If that brand lives and dies with you, what happens to that trust when you're unavailable?

Too many brokers operate under the illusion that they're only responsible for their own output, but leadership and legacy come with a broader duty. Legacy isn't a vanity project or a personal milestone. It's a form of stewardship. It's your opportunity to ensure that what you're building continues to create value, even in your absence. A sellable business is a resilient business, and resilience isn't just smart; it's ethical. It's how you honor the people who have invested their time, trust, and talent in you. That's how you build a legacy that matters.

Designing for Legacy

Designing a business worth selling doesn't mean you have to sell it. It means you've created optionality: the freedom to choose what comes next, on your terms. Maybe your children will want to step in. Maybe a partner will buy you out. Maybe a competitor or consolidator will make an offer you can't ignore. Or maybe you'll choose to step back entirely, collect dividends, and watch your leadership team run the show. But none of these options exist if your business still depends on your name, your presence, and your constant involvement.

Legacy isn't built at the exit. It's built years before, and it comes down to how intentional you are today in separating your business from yourself. Here are a few foundational strategies for designing a legacy-ready business:

- **Brand beyond yourself:** Develop a company identity that can thrive without your personal name or reputation at the center. Your brand should stand for something bigger than you.

- **Document everything:** Standard Operating Procedures are the blueprint for continuity. If someone else can't follow your systems without calling you, they aren't real systems.

- **Build a leadership bench:** Train and empower others to lead, sell, and make decisions. True leadership is measured not by how much you do but by how well others perform when you step away.

- **Measure what matters:** Track the metrics that signal health and value like profitability, client experience, pipeline stability, conversion rates, and cost of client acquisition. These are the KPIs buyers and future leaders will care about.

Designing for legacy means building something that can outlast you. Something that can scale, evolve, and endure with or without your involvement. At the end of the day, legacy isn't just about how things end, but about what you've built along the way. You can run a successful mortgage business for 10, 15, or even 20 years and still have nothing to sell at the end of it. Or, you can build with intention from the start—creating systems, empowering people, and designing for scale—and end up with something that continues to pay you long after you've stepped away.

The best part? It's never too late to begin. No matter where you are on your journey, you still have time to restructure your business, develop your team, and put the right foundations in place. You still have time to build something that can last, whether you plan to pass it on, step back, or eventually sell. The decision is yours. So ask yourself: What kind of legacy are you building?

Free Download: Legacy Roadmap

For a free downloadable roadmap to plan your legacy—balancing financial, lifestyle, and community impact, go to: dougadlam.com/brokering

Or scan the QR code below:

Conclusion

When I wrote the introduction to this book, I shared how I entered the mortgage industry without a roadmap, but with deep preparation and a clear intention to build something meaningful. If you've made it to this final chapter, then I imagine you're wired the same way. You care about more than just volume. You want to grow in a way that's aligned with your values, your vision, and your life.

Throughout these pages, we've explored the core building blocks of a sellable, sustainable, and high-performing mortgage business. We've looked at branding and brokerage models, leadership and succession, client experience and compliance, data and transparency. But underneath it all is a single truth:

Success in this industry isn't about doing everything right; it's about doing the *right* things with *purpose.*

That might mean asking hard questions; choosing the business model that fits your life, not someone else's; leading with transparency, not ego; and scaling through systems, not burnout. Above all, be sure to remember that the decisions you make today aren't just about growth. They're about longevity.

The mortgage business is always changing. Regulatory shifts, compensation changes, technology disruptions—they're not going away. But the professionals who thrive are the ones who remain steady in the face of that change. Not because they resist it, but because they've built something resilient enough to adapt. That's what I hope this book helps you do:

Build a business that can scale without you and build a life that feels more aligned because of it.

However, this isn't the end of your journey. It's just another beginning. And wherever you go next, know this: The mortgage industry needs more high-integrity leaders.

Let's be those leaders—together.

About the Author

Doug Adlam

Doug Adlam is a nationally recognized entrepreneur, speaker, and strategic advisor in Canada's mortgage and financial industries. With a career spanning over 17 years, Doug has co-founded and exited multiple ventures, including an industry disrupting mortgage technology, Finmo, that was acquired by Lendesk in 2020.

Doug began his journey by growing his family's mortgage brokerage, Champion Mortgage, 40X. Later he went on to serve as Director of Strategic Growth for Axiom (later rebranded Indi Mortgage), and played a pivotal role in scaling it into a national powerhouse—quadrupling its operations in just two and a half years and helping lead it to billions in annual originations. He also co-founded a successful wealth management startup focused on corporate financial planning, which he exited in 2023.

A former professor at the University of Guelph, Doug taught marketing, consumer behaviour, and information management for six years and founded the university's Entrepreneurship 4100 course. He holds an Honours Bachelor of Commerce in Marketing Management and a post-graduate degree in Marketing and Consumer Studies, following an early academic start in Computer Systems Engineering.

Today, Doug is the founder of Adlam Innovations, a strategic platform focused on helping leaders scale businesses that operate—and eventually exit—without them. He is a sought-after keynote speaker, podcast guest, and advisor to founders, executives, and high-growth teams.

To learn more, visit DougAdlam.com.